TRAINING MA

for

TRAINING METHODS

2000 Edition

Professor William Krug
Professor Janet Achor

Vernon Dahlstrom (Contributing Author)
Susan Ahlersmeyer (Contributing Author)

Department of Organizational Leadership
Purdue University

Learning Systems, INC.
Custom Publishing Division
531 Carrolton Boulevard
West Lafayette, IN 47906

765.497.6447

INDEX OF CONTENTS

OLS 375
TEAM ROSTER

Team Number: _____ Division: _____ Section: _____

Team Leader: _____ Phone #: _____

Team Members _____ Phone #: _____

_____   _____

_____   _____

_____   _____

_____   _____

_____   _____

Group Project Title: _____

Group Project Presentation Date: _____

Enviremental - requirements
Seating + set-up

40 mins. / 12-20 break / repeat process
teaching /

Oct 28th   7:30
Nov. 1st.
Apollo American

P.3
   Chapter 1
       Hard-Rock Cafe   35-50 yrs.
          Younger group
Competitive training / success of individual / Job satisfaction
Continuous training / tuition assistance
Training / part of business strategie
      TQM

P.4 Training - create inteligent Capital -
Long

— Make yourself obsolete-
85% jobs will require knowledge

— Benchmarking— propietory
Continuous learning - little pieces, big picture, reassurance

P.5 Importance of Training   5% payroll

P.6 Seven Steps.
       readiness
P.8 Concept - pretesting
P.9 forces that effect training / training
       85% do not have global skills
P.10 succesion planing ; employee / mentoring
      empowering
P.12 (1.2) resource occupational
      service / fast
P.13 38% interaction
P.19 T.Q.M.   Over

P.17 botton, population
  .18 race, gender, immgrants recyling
      communications
P..21 COTS training progams P.22 virtual teams
P.25 Fig 1.3 training quality ? chart
P 30 organization of book chapters

6+13 Decm
29 Nov.

chapter 2
P.39 capital
  .40 Ed Com
      250 courses to employees
      tuition assistance

P41 & 42 S.W.O.T.
P45 business
           2.3 saturation

P46 provide more
P.47 staff to stradegies
P.49 support
.50 knowledge is power
      sharing

1. Scan
2. Focus
3. acts

FOUR PHASES OF OLS 375

Phase I	Phase II
Analysis Phase	**Development Phase**
Needs Analysis	Learner Objectives
Task Analysis	Trainee Evaluations
Learner Analysis	Instructional Sequence
Training Proposal	Script
	Story Board
	Rough Draft
Phase III	**Phase IV**
Delivery Phase	**Revision/Evaluation Phase**
Final Trainer Manual	Program Evaluation
Final Trainee Manual	Program Revision
Video	
Pilot Test Program	

P. 55 S.W.O.T.
Strenghs weakness / opportunities Threats (Learned something new)
internal | external
possibilities

P. 62 virtual training
would, could, should of club
on the job training removing obstacles, take care of them
Manager to Trainee
product design, quality

P. 64 problems / one sided

INTRODUCTION TO TRAINING METHODS

The development of training follows a step-by-step sequence of events from initial awareness of a performance problem area to the development and delivery of training and the evaluation of its effectiveness. This Training Manual will take your through the step-by-step principles, practices and methods of employee training. The Systematic Design to development of a training program involves four steps: analysis, development, evaluation, and presentation/revision. Emphasis in this course is on the supervisor as a trainer. This is a practical approach to problem solving using training as one method to resolve an employee performance discrepancy.

Training Design Flow Chart

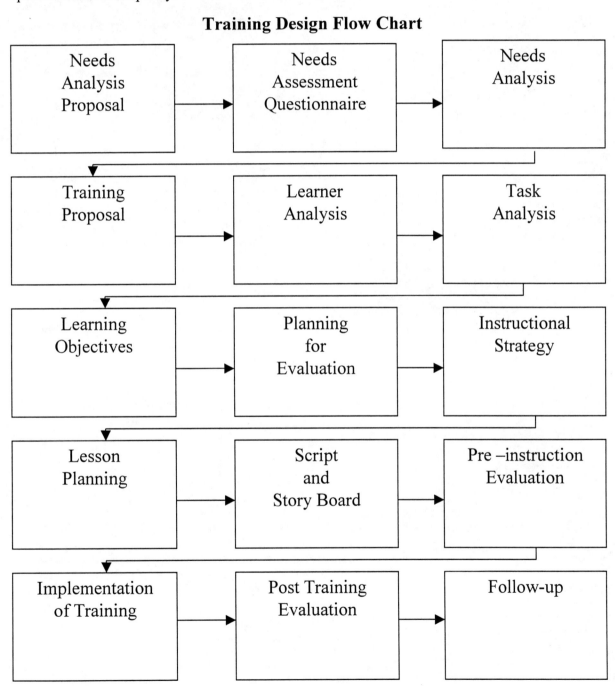

OLS 375 Possible Training Topics

Management & Supervision (Soft skill training)
- Leadership Skills - *Interpersonal*
    - How to Conduct Interviews Effectively
    - Training Supervisors on ADA
    - Workplace Violence Prevention Training
    - Benefits Training for New Employees
    - New Employee Orientation
    - Sales Associate Training

Customer Service (Soft skill training for people)
- Calming Upset Customers
- Providing Quality Service (Basic Techniques of)
- Seeing the Customer's point of View (Listening Skills)

Technical & Safety (Providing technical information on something)
- Computer Skills
- How to read Blueprints
- Hearing and Sight Protection
- Ladder Safety
- Equipment Operation (Set up and operate)
- CPR Training (Only if you are a certified instructor)
- Wellness Programs
    - Exercise and Stress Management
    - Back Certification
    - How to Take Blood Pressure

Miscellaneous (How to skills work well in a training program)
- How to Set up and Operate a Cam Recorder
- How to Assemble a Bike
- How to Write a Resume
- Tire Changing Skills
- Nurses Aid Training – Taking vital signs
- How to Improve Your Golf Stroke

Computer Training
- New Hire Computer Orientation
- Clip Art Training
- How to Develop a Power Point Presentation
- How to Develop Your Own Web Page

Aviation
- Standard Pre-flight Procedures
- How to Fuel an Airplane
- How to Hanger and De-hanger an Airplane
- Flight Planning

Special project opportunities – volunteer to develop a training program for where you work or to support a non-profit organization.

FROM IDEA TO PROGRAM

HERE'S HOW TO HELP CLIENTS SOLVE PROBLEMS — AND BE A HERO.

BY PHILLIP J. STELLA

Fade up on medium shot of Biff, the bright young video producer for Foonman Industries, sitting behind his cluttered desk. Cut to close-up as the phone rings:

Biff: Corporate video, this is Biff, how can I help you?

Ralph: Hi, Biff, this is Ralph over in marketing. Listen, Biff, I need a 15-minute video made for next week's sales conference. How much will it cost, and how long will it take?

Zoom in on Biff's annoyed expression. Dissolve to medium shot as Biff mutters under his breath and pulls a bottle of aspirin from his drawer.

Ralph: Biff — Hello — Are you there?

If this scene is too real or a frequent experience for you, then read on. Here is a video primer in pre-production — what's involved in planning a successful video. Although it is aimed at producers, it is also for your clients, the Ralphs of this world. It can help you help them solve their communication problems, aiming at that bottom line: happy clients, excellent results and a video producer who becomes a hero.

Experience teaches us the importance of the essential pre-production stage; planning is everything in video. That's where most of the mistakes happen and where most lessons are learned. Failing to plan is planning to fail. Producers new to the field and battle-weary veterans can benefit from some valuable tips.

Problem-solving

At the core of the process is *Lesson Learned No. 1:* You're a problem-solver, not a video producer. You produce videos, but your real goal is to help clients solve prob-

---

Stella is president of Effective Training & Communication, Cleveland, and a founding member of the Cleveland chapter of the ITVA.

---

16 LESSONS LEARNED

Lesson No. 1:
You're a problem-solver, not a video producer.

Lesson No. 2:
Analyze the problem.

Lesson No. 3:
Identify your audience.

Lesson No. 4:
Tone can overshadow content.

Lesson No. 5:
Video isn't a panacea.

Lesson No. 6:
Create viewer-based objectives.

Lesson No. 7:
Video is rarely the total solution.

Lesson No. 8:
Strive for the best approach.

Lesson No. 9:
Clarify sign-offs up front.

Lesson No. 10:
Prepare a thorough budget estimate, and avoid budget surprises.

Lesson No. 11:
It will always take more time and money than you planned.

Lesson No. 12:
The script is everything.

Lesson No. 13:
Involve clients as much as they need and want to be.

Lesson No. 14:
Always expect the unexpected.

Lesson No. 15:
You can't always fix it in post.

Lesson No. 16:
It's not over until the paperwork is done.

> THE MORE YOU KNOW ABOUT THE AUDIENCE, THE BETTER YOU'LL BE ABLE TO COMMUNICATE SUCCESSFULLY WITH ITS MEMBERS.

lems. Video is a tool that you use: it is a means to an end, not an end in itself.

It all begins with that phone call from "Ralph." Clients often think they know how to solve their problems before you've helped them determine what the problems are. So let's begin pre-production planning with *Lesson Learned No. 2: Analyze the problem.* The next time "Ralph" calls, already on step No. 10, try to move him back to the beginning to precisely define the problem. Ask specific questions:
• What problem are you trying to solve? What are the symptoms?
• What is its frequency or severity? How many people are affected?
• What is the problem's cost? What happens if you don't solve it? Such problem definition, even if it is only subjective, lends credibility to the process and to the solution.

"The answers to these basic questions usually drive how I advise and guide clients," commented Dave Phillips, manager of video communications at TRW. And Don Stephens, TV facility manager at Goodyear, added, "Often, you need to probe for details to get past their preconceived notions."

Audience

The more you know about the audience, the better you'll be able to communicate successfully with its members. But *Lesson Learned No. 3 — Identify your audience —* isn't just limited to demographics. Of course, you need to know about the viewers. Who are they? How many? What is their average age? What are their job functions and levels?

However, of equal importance is the viewing environment:
• What is the type of viewing location? What is the average audience size?

• Is viewing the program required or optional? Will it be viewed at work or at home? Individual or small group? Is it structured or unstructured?

Also, examine the audience's attitudes:
• How does the audience feel about the topic now? How do you want them to feel about it after the video?
• How does the audience feel about the messenger (the company) and the medium (video)?

Any large audience is a difficult target to hit. "It's better to use a rifle instead of a shotgun to zero in on specific segments within a larger group," advised Ken Jurek, director of video and communications for Management Recruiters International (MRI), an executive search organization.

Therefore, try to determine whether there are important "hidden viewers," those people whose opinions are critical to the success of the project. Those hidden audiences might be higher management, regulatory or governmental agencies, union officials or public interest groups, and they may need to be politically appeased in the process. If you're leading your client through a mine field, it helps if you know where the mines are buried.

Also, Stephens warns against trying to use the same video for employees and customers. Each group has different information needs and interests.

Next, determine the tone or feel — the subjective psychological effect the message should have on the audience. Heed the warning of *Lesson Learned No. 4: Tone can overshadow content.* Help your client choose a tone appropriate to the message and audience. How the message is conveyed will influence viewers' attitudes about content and the messenger.

> THE ONLY THING WORSE THAN A BAD VIDEO IS A GOOD VIDEO THAT SHOULD HAVE BEEN A MEMO, MEETING OR NEWSLETTER ARTICLE INSTEAD.

Alternatives

By now, you've determined the problem, audience and tone of the message. Before continuing, you must do something that is foreign to many video professionals: Help your client decide if there are effective alternative solutions that are faster, better or cheaper than video. Ask why they have chosen video. Although it may seem that you're turning away business, remember Lesson Learned No. 1. Although you may lose some business, you'll gain the client's respect and confidence. And there's always next time.

The only thing worse than a bad video is a good video that should have been a memo, meeting or newsletter article instead. Even the hard core among us will admit to *Lesson Learned No. 5*: Video isn't a panacea. It isn't the only solution to communication problems, and sometimes it's not even a good one.

"If video isn't the most appropriate, I always suggest alternatives," said Marc Bakst, video manager at Lorain County Community College (LCCC), Elyria, OH. "An audiocassette might be much better than a long, boring talking head with no visuals or graphics."

Objectives

Once you and your client have decided on the use of video, you must deal with *Lesson Learned No. 6*: Create viewer-based objectives. "Sometimes you really need to probe," said Jurek. "You play devil's advocate with a client to help determine what the video is trying to accomplish."

Determine objectives that are clear, specific, achievable, viewer-based and measurable. Although skill objectives ("The viewers will be able to do ...") are easier to deal with than knowledge objectives ("The viewers will understand the importance of ..."), most videos include both.

Measurability is important when you evaluate the results of the video. Jurek sends out brief evaluation cards with each program sold to franchises. Of 3,000 viewers, often 50% respond that they analyze the feedback by computer and regularly use the input and ideas, and that they often call people to follow up on specific comments.

LCCC's Bakst observed, "It is difficult to accurately gauge a video's effectiveness, especially if it is combined with other media. It's very subjective." Goodyear's Stephens doesn't always give program evaluation the attention it deserves, sometimes settling for the happiness of the client and the client's boss.

Campaign

The next step is to help your client determine the video's relationship to other communication elements involved in solving the problem. Warn the client about *Lesson Learned No. 7*: Video is rarely the total solution.

• Will there be handouts, meeting visuals, newsletters or other support?

• Will video initiate the message or reinforce a message previously delivered by other methods?

• Will video provide the big picture or the detailed, step-by-step instruction?

• Will there be discussion, handouts, workbooks, testing, exercises or other learning activities?

For best results, help your client create a multifaceted communication campaign. Video may be the primary element, but it should work harmoniously with print support and other tools to effectively deliver, expand, clarify, personalize and sufficiently reinforce the message.

Parameters

Now it's time to pin down production parameters, just as *Lesson Learned No. 8* urges: Strive for the best approach. Avoid always using the first one you think of or the one you usually think of. Help your client determine the various elements:

• Format: Will you use talking heads? A documentary format? Dramatization or narrative?

• Length: Most corporate videos produced today are less than 20 minutes long, with many less than 15 minutes. Avoid running so long that you lose viewer interest. Phillips warned. "The typical viewer at home can watch television for about 12 minutes before needing a snack or bathroom break." When longer content is necessary, he often suggests modules or a multipart series to keep the actual video segment time short.

• Talent: Political considerations notwithstanding, professional talent adds quality and credibility to your message. In-house people should do what they do best — the role of content expert or newsmaker. They are rarely successful in the uncomfortable role of news presenter.

• Production resources: Based on project needs, budget limitations and available in-house resources, recommend the best approach to your client. If you don't have the time, talent or capacity to do the project in-house, recommend outside services or free-lancers.

• Task/time list: Given the above considerations, develop a detailed list of who is to do what by when. Emphasize the client's important role at key points in the process.

• Sign-offs: Heed *Lesson Learned No. 9*: Clarify sign-offs up front. Who will sign off on the proposal, script, rough cut and final cut? Stress the danger of presuming too much authority and of asking for forgiveness instead of permission. Allow sign-off in your timeline. A client's boss should be involved, but Jurek advises against decisions by committee wherever possible.

Another important consideration is the budget. Although practices vary greatly among companies, one practice should be constant: Prepare a thorough budget estimate, and avoid budget surprises — *Lesson Learned No. 10*. Keep your client informed about actual expenses as the project progresses, and communicate the effect that changes (whether unforeseen or client-driven) will have on overall costs and completion time. Closely related is *Lesson Learned No. 11*: It will always take more time and money than you planned.

The script is everything, according to *Lesson Learned No. 12*. "Although creative production values can make a good script even better, it's difficult — if not impossible — to make a good video out of a bad script," said Bakst. The detailed needs analysis is a good start, but the script must still be outlined, researched, written, polished and signed off. If clients want to write the script themselves, stress the logic of allowing you or a competent free-lancer to sculpt and polish it.

Production

Once in production, several considerations can affect your results, regardless of your resources or limitations:

• *Lesson Learned No. 13*: Involve clients as much as they need and want to be. Although shoots and edit sessions can go smoother without clients around, it makes sense for them to see this complex process first-hand. The more they understand, the more they'll appreciate how difficult it is and how good you are at it. Also, although clients can learn by observation, "some clients don't want to be involved — or can't," said Jurek. "They trust us to do a professional job. That's why we're in business."

• *Lesson Learned No. 14*: Always expect the unexpected. You can't plan the timing or nature of crises, but you can plan how to deal with them when they occur. Equipment, weather, talent, facilities or crew members can be the root of the problem. Always have a contingency plan in mind.

• *Lesson Learned No. 15*: You can't always fix it in post. Don't assume that clever use of special effects, editing or graphics can mask production shortcomings. A thorough shot sheet and storyboard will help you avoid production errors or oversights.

• *Lesson Learned No. 16*: It's not over until the paperwork is done. Before popping the champagne cork, take care of needed paperwork. Write a project summary for your client, comparing budget estimates with actual costs and detailing those variances. Thank the client for the support, help, cooperation, involvement, patience and/or confidence, as applicable. Indicate what you both learned from the process to make the next one faster, better or cheaper. After all, you want the client to bring you another project, don't you?

You're ready

Borrowing from Vince Lombardi, "Planning isn't the most important thing; it's the only thing." By now you can see the wisdom of thorough pre-production and effective communications with your client. Use your video resources to help solve your client's problems, meet or exceed their expectations and become a hero in the process.

Now, sit back, put your feet up on your desk, and wait for "Ralph" to call. ▼

THE KEY STEPS IN PRE-PRODUCTION

• Analyze the problem

• Identify your audience

Introduction to Needs Analysis:

Special Rush Orders Case

The Acme Supply Company is a medium-sized organization that supplies mechanical supplies to a number of manufacturing companies located in the southwestern part of the United States. The company employs 30 salespeople whose job it is to contact customers in the field, sell them on the products, and maintain and service the contract over a number of years.

Each sales employee undergoes extensive training by the company covering effective prospecting and sales techniques as well as standard operating procedures. The company's training program places considerable emphasis on its ordering procedures. Upon receiving an order, each salesperson is to designate on the order form if the order is "normal" or a "special rush order." A "normal" order,, which applies to most purchases, is filled and delivered within 7 to 10 days. A "special rush order" is one that applies to emergency situations (one in which the customer needs a product very quickly) or to customers who buy merchandise as a result of special company promotions. It is delivered within 2 – 3 days. A "special rush order" requires the individual attention of one of the stockroom employees and hence disrupts the overall coordination of the searching and compiling involved in filling the many daily orders. An employee must search out the products in the stockroom, compile each order, and move it to a central disbursal point for distribution.

One week Ron Taylor, one of the executive vice presidents of Acme, was visiting with Mike Russell, the order complier who receives the nightly phone orders from the salespeople. While they were visiting, Paul Conway, one of Acme's most successful salespeople, called in five orders, three of which were labeled "special rush." He said he would bring in the order forms the next day. Later in the week, Ron was talking with Grant Pierson, one of Acme's better accounts. In the course of the conversation, Grant said, "I certainly like dealing with you man, Paul Conway. He always fills my orders in a minimum of time. That man knows how to deal with customers.

The situation bothered Ron because, while he was pleased that Grant had a high regard for Paul, he wondered whether the "special rush order" procedure was being abused. Further investigation confirmed Ron's suspicion. Not only was Paul marking many orders "special rush" but so also were the other salespeople. Ron's investigation also revealed that the "normal" orders were now taking 11-14 days to fill rather than 7 – 10 days.

Discussion Questions:

1. What is the problem from an organizational perspective?

2. Is the company's training program at fault for what happened in this case? How do you know for sure?

3. Does anyone need further training? If so, who and what should be the nature of the training?

4. What action do you recommend Ron Taylor take in this case?

5. Will peer pressure eventually produce a change in Paul's behavior?

6. What do you need to make a decision in this case?

NEEDS ANALYSIS PROPOSAL
(I think there is a performance problem, now how do I get permission to study it?)

When a supervisor becomes aware of a potential performance problem area and wants to investigate it further it is often necessary to notify management prior to further investigation of the problem in order to facilitate the correct allocation of resources. The Needs Analysis Proposal is one way to notify management of this potential problem. It is a one-page memo that may request money, facilities, time, manpower, etc., to properly assess this problem. Or, it may simply ask permission or inform the reader of the problem and that you will be working to solve it. The proposal can be addressed to your boss, client, the president of the organization, or whoever is appropriate. For this class if no one else is appropriate, address the proposal to your instructor.

The first step is to put yourself in the reader's position and determine what information the reader will need to make a decision. The following table will take you through the thought process of the reader.

A typical proposal is written in memorandum format and has five sections: heading, opening, summary, discussion, and closing.

Section	Your reader's questions	Your answer
Heading	What is this?	To: Name From: Name Date: M,D,Y Subj: Proposal...
Opening	What is it about?	Problem you're trying to solve. Task or description of what you are proposing. Purpose of this memo.
Summary	What is in it for me?	My goals are... Will benefit you this way.
Discussion	How will you do this? When will it be done? What will it cost? Why should I listen to you?	Your plan, equipment needed, schedule and your qualifications.
Closing	What do you want from me? How will I get in touch with you?	Request reader's permission or approval. Reach me at...
Attachments (optional)	I want to know more...?	See attachments

The opening, summary, discussion, and closing sections are concise paragraphs addressing the questions shown above.

See the following page for more information on each paragraph.

The following guidelines will help you determine what should go in each paragraph of your Needs Analysis Proposal. Remember to write this in memo format. Be convincing and to the point.

Paragraph # 1: **The Opening Statement.** The opening statement tells your reader exactly why you are writing and what you are proposing. **At this point, you are recommending an assessment to determine what the problem is and whether or not training is one of the solutions.** Be sure the word "Proposal" appears toward the beginning. Address the problem as you see it, what you are proposing to do about it, and the purpose of the memo. Remember at this stage you do not know if training is a solution yet.

Paragraph # 2: **The Summary Statement.** This paragraph is devoted to explaining the performance problem as you currently see it and why it is important enough to warrant further investigation. Then address the assessment in terms of its importance to the organization. There are two parts to this section: benefits and features. Address both areas in terms that your reader can understand. **Empower the reader to accept your idea.**

Paragraph # 3: **The Discussion Statement.** This paragraph is devoted to how you plan to assess the situation, methods and means. Include a rough time table and an estimate of costs. Also tell your reader why you are qualified to do this project. This is important because it will help management assess whether you are the best person to do the assessment.

Paragraph # 4: **The Closing Statement.** This last paragraph answers the question, "Now what?" Spell out explicitly who is responsible for the next move, if you need permission to move further then state so, if you need resources then request them. Too many proposals fail at this point because they are not clear as to who is responsible for what.

Some Suggestions:

Organize your ideas according to your reader's interests. If your reader is concerned about cost, don't bury it. If he or she is concerned about benefits, highlight them.

Use single-theme paragraphs. This writing technique will increase your clarity.

Strive for one-page proposals. No one has time to read long proposals, so keep it short. With each additional page you diminish your chances of being read and remembered.

Don't become a slave to this model. Each communication is unique. Use this model as a guide and starting point, not as a written-in-stone formula.

Take a logical look at what you have written, and ask yourself--Is everything explained to a point that the reader can make a decision?

Remember that managers are busy people so present a clear concise picture of what is happening, why it is important, and what you would like to do about it.

See examples next page:

NEEDS ANALYSIS PROPOSAL EXAMPLE

To: Lynn Hallstein, Clerical Pool Supervisor
From: Elrene Barnard, Director of Training
Date: October 21, 1999
Subject: Proposal to study possible secretarial skills training

The purpose of this proposal is to recommend an assessment of possible secretarial skills training. As we discussed earlier, the problems of maintaining a good secretarial staff are not new. You mentioned a constant problem in the hiring and retaining of qualified secretaries, as well as paying fees to personnel agencies to find secretaries as needed. I am proposing a study of our secretarial training to identify possible problem areas with a look toward solving them.

If training deficiencies can be identified, then a training program could be developed to correct them. The possible benefits of a training program for your department are numerous:

1.   Dollar savings in agency fees

2.   Increased efficiency and productivity

3.   Decreased turnover

4.   Improved morale by providing a career path to workers

5.   Preparation for office-automated systems

I would like to conduct a needs analysis assessment with current secretarial staff and to interview three to five key managers. Cost will be limited due to the small number of personnel being surveyed. This data will be used to determine if training is the most cost-effective solution. If so, a secretarial skills training program will be developed. I will be prepared to complete the needs analysis by November 12 and should be able to begin the training by early next year.

I need your cooperation to begin the project. I will call on Monday to set up a meeting so we can discuss your reactions to the proposal and confirm the start-up date.

Sincerely,

Your signature

Remember: Do not yet assume training is the solution! Training is one of the many options you'll be exploring. Think about the problem using Mager's flow chart as an approach to analyzing the problem.

NEEDS ASSESSMENT STRATEGIES
(What questions do I ask and how do I ask them?)

A Needs Assessment Survey is a tool used to collect data concerning possible problems and solutions. FOCUS ON THE LEARNER. Surveys using different types of questions are used to ask the learner to identify specific needs for which you are looking for a solution. Keep an open mind. Having a preconceived notion can easily keep you from finding the real cause and/or solution to a performance problem.

When doing a Needs Assessment work from a model of human performance and develop an assessment tool that will clearly identify the performance problem and it causes. A training needs assessment is a systematic method for determining what needs to be done to bring performance in a particular job, or set of jobs to the expected level. Keep in mind that a performance discrepancy might be caused by faulty equipment or procedures, and might mot be poor worker performance.

Framework for Training Needs Analysis:

PD(Performance discrepancy) = EP(Expected performance-AP(Actual performance)

Assessment covers the following three areas:

Organization Analysis- involves looking at the internal environment of the organization and determining its fit with organizational goals and objectives. Examines how these factors affect job performance and constraints on possible training.

Should include the following:
- An examination of the mission and strategies of an organization
- An examination of the resources and allocation of resources, given the objectives
- An analysis of the factors in the internal environment to determine if they are causing the problem
- If training is required, the impact of those environmental factors on providing training and transferring the training to the job.

Operational (Task) Analysis- examines specific jobs to determine the requirements of Knowledge, Skills and Attitudes (KSA's) that are necessary to get the job done.
- Worker oriented approach, focuses on the Knowledge, Skills and Attitudes (KSA's) that are required on the job, rather that the tasks or behaviors.
- Task oriented approach identifies the various work activities required to perform the job.

What you should get from the job analysis (expected performance)
- Knowledge – declarative knowledge, knowledge requirements necessary to be successful
- Skill – a list of all skill requirements to perform the job successfully.

- <u>Attitudes</u> –attitudes and feelings necessary to perform the job successfully.

Validity = is the degree to which you are measuring what you want to measure

Reliability = is the consistency of a measure.

Person Analysis (Learner Analysis) examines those who occupy the job to see if they have the required KSA's to do the job.

Components of Needs Assessment:

Actual = what is happening

Expected = what should be happening

Cause = Why does the problem exist?

Symptoms = what are the effects of the problem. (This is what we normally see)

** Always remember that the only effective solution to any problem must address it cause. **

Causes:
1. A deficiency of knowledge – do not know how to perform or what results to seek.
2. A deficiency of environment (deficiency of execution)
3. A combination of the two.

**Human Performance depends upon:
- Knowing what is expected and having the KSA's to do it
- Feedback system is place to let me know how I am doing.

Instructional Solutions
- Only when performance problems are caused by deficiencies in individual knowledge, skills and attitudes
- Other alternative have been ruled out

Training Needs Assessment Questions
- What is the discrepancy or gap (what is and what ought to be)
- Is the need (discrepancy) documented anywhere?
- What are the consequences if the need is not met?
- What caused the need to be brought to your attention at this time?
- Is it a training problem? Motivation? Or an environmental problem?

Setting up a needs assessment plan;
- Set objective or desired results
- Target you audience
- Determine sampling procedures
- Select data collection methods
- Write specification for instruments

- Methods of data analysis
- How will decisions be made based on the data

Designing and Implementing the Needs Assessment:

A variety of needs assessment tools are available for use with your choice depending upon the specific problem, the organization, and the people. Some of the more common methods are:

Informal interview	Observation	Survey
Performance tests	Formal interview	Company reports
Record examinations	Advisory committee	Checklists
Questionnaires	Formal research	Industry standards

Some typical types of questions that you might use in an assessment:

Broad general questions.

"What problems have you recently had on the job?"
(This type of question opens all possible causes as to why performance is not what is should be.)

Ask learners to express priorities among possible topics or skills that might be included in a training course.

"Rate each of the following skills in terms of your need to improve your effectiveness in the...?"
(Gets employee input on areas that might help them improve performance.)

Ask learners to demonstrate particular skills, as a kind of pretest.

"Write the following sentence in shorthand."
(Designed to get an assessment of actual performance.)

Ask the learners questions that attempt to uncover the feelings that they have about a particular course or skill.

"How interested would you be in a workshop on ...?"

Ask learners to identify what they think are the best solutions to a problem.

"It has been found that many people are not receiving their office messages or understanding them. How would you improve our office communication?"

This last question empowers the employee to look at any possible option that might improve performance. This could identify solutions that might be more cost- effective than instruction.

Nine Basic Needs Assessment Methods

Tool	Advantages	Disadvantages
Observation	Minimizes interruption Situational data	Need a skilled observer Employee feels spied upon
Questionnaire	Inexpensive Can use on large audience	Limited free ideas Low response rate
Key employee consultation	Simple and inexpensive Employee's own perspective	Built in bias Only get partial view
Print Media	Easily available Good for normative needs	Data does not match your situation
Interviews	Good for feelings, causes and possible solutions. Empowers employee	Time consuming Difficult to analyze
Group Interviews	Different viewpoints Low individual response	Time consuming Difficult to synthesize
Performance Tests	Helpful to determine a knowledge or skill problem	Validity is an issue
Work records and reports	Clues to trouble spots Easy to collect	Problems or solutions might not show up
Work Samples	Is organization's own data Provides good clues	Takes time from job Needs specialized content analysis

22

Needs Assessment Survey of OLS 375 Class

1. **What problems have you had in preparing written assignments for class?**

_____

_____

_____

_____

2. **Rate the following equipment in terms of your ability to use that equipment:**
   (Circle your answer)   Skill level (5 = highly skilled, 1 = no skills)

Typewriter	5	4	3	2	1
Electronic word processor	5	4	3	2	1
Computer word processor	5	4	3	2	1

3. **Demonstrate your ability to proof your written work by correcting the following paragraph:**

   John BLAIR the personal manager at Purdue a mediun sized university was told by the president that they had just received a large contract from the united States Department of agriculture to develop a farm safety course. Since the contract was for 5,000,000 $'s John has decided to hire some new personal to do the work and has asked for you help. What help due think you can give. Respond to me ASAP.

4. **How interested would you be in a workshop on the following: (circle your answer)**
   Interest (5 = very interested, 1 = no interest)

Grammar and spelling	5	4	3	2	1
Business writing format	5	4	3	2	1
Using Word for Windows	5	4	3	2	1
Into to Computer Labs	5	4	3	2	1

5. **Over the past 3 years the quality of homework assignments has not been as high as it should be. How would you improve the quality of homework assignments?**

_____

_____

_____

Needs Assessment Exercise on Teaming

1. What problems have you had in your team meetings?

_____

_____

_____

2. Rate the following team member responsibilities in terms of your skill to perform: (circle your answer)

	Skill Level (5=highest, 1= no skill)				

Voice my opinion on the topic being discussed.	5	4	3	2	1
Confine my opinion to the specific assignment topic.	5	4	3	2	1
Demonstrate appreciation for other's point of view.	5	4	3	2	1
Accept and support consensus decisions of the team.	5	4	3	2	1
Prepare for team meetings by completing each homework assignment.	5	4	3	2	1

3. Demonstrate your ability to deal with team conflicts by offering a solution for the following situation:

Joan Bannon is a team leader for a production crew at IBM. Her team meets every Monday to discuss the obstacles each person ran into during the prior week in performing their daily work assignments. Lately, the weekly team meetings have resulted in heated verbal exchanges between the same two members. It appears that they simply enjoy arguing for the sake of arguing, and not that they genuinely differ in how they think a specific obstacle should be handled. Other team members have mentioned to Joan that they want to transfer to another production team because of this weekly conflict.

What can Joan do to effectively deal with this situation? _____

_____

_____

4. How interested would you be in a class session covering a topic related to team building skills? (circle you answer)

    Very Interested   _Kind of Interested_   _Little Interest_   _No Interest_

5. What ideas do you have that might make your team meetings more productive?

_____

_____

_____

_____

NEEDS ASSESSMENT QUESTIONNAIRE WORKSHEET

What method or methods would you use to administer this questionnaire? _____

_____

Broad general question: _____

_____

_____

Question concerning learners' priorities as to possible topics or skills for training:

_____

_____

_____

Demonstration of a skill or knowledge area: _____

_____

_____

_____

Question to determine the learner's feelings about a particular training area: _____

_____

_____

_____

Question to get learner's idea as to how to solve a particular problem: _____

_____

_____

_____

NEEDS ANALYSIS
Also referred to as a Gap Analysis
(A way to capture and make sense of what you have found out about this problem from your Needs Assessment.)

A Needs Analysis is an analytical tool used to determine the needs of an organization. **It focuses on the differences between the way work should be done and the way work is actually done.** The purpose of a needs analysis is to identify, define, document, justify and prioritize these differences or gaps in results. These gaps are called <u>performance deficiencies.</u>

The process of conducting a needs analysis involves five steps:

1. Identify performance standards
2. Assess current performance

3. Identify gaps

4. Prioritize for action

5. Develop a strategy to close gaps

I.   DESIRED PERFORMANCES -Your Needs Assessment Questionnaire has identified a problem area. Part of the task of determining how bad a problem is is to identify the desired (competent) performance that you are looking for keeping in mind a consideration for organizational goals. In addition to this look at other related aspects of this area that this person might be required to do at work. EXAMPLE: you are training a sales person to change the oil in their company car. He or she also needs to know (1) why it is important to change the oil, (2) knowing when to change the oil, (3) what the company policy is as to car maintenance. These would all relate to a situation where car maintenance is required. DO NOT BREAK DOWN what you are going to train (how to change oil in a car) into smaller steps. That will be done when we do a Task Analysis!

In addition to identifying four different aspects of the job, specify how well you want the person to know and/or do <u>each</u> job. Specifying how well you want each person to do each job is called the "standards of performance." <u>Quantify</u> these desired results in numerical terms. This will take some effort on your part because many times we do not think in these terms, but it CAN be done. SOME words leave too much to interpretation, i.e., "correct (ly), proper (ly), good, appropriate, the right amount," and so on. AVOID these. Some better examples of standards of performance are:

1. With no errors (or without errors)

2. Nine out of ten times (or eight out of ten, or three out of four, etc.)

3. 95 percent (or 85, or 90, or even 100)

4. No more than .002 tolerances, or deviation from the identified standard

5. Close the cash drawer with not over 10+ deviations from tape total in balancing

6. Greet customers within thirty seconds of entering the store

7. Begin filling order within fifteen seconds of taking it

8. Mail a response within 24 hours of receiving request

9. <u>Always</u> greet customers with a smile

10. Be present and ready to assist customers at <u>all</u> times

<u>Remember</u>: **Each job needs a specific standard of performance identified.**

II. <u>ASSESS CURRENT PERFORMANCE</u> -You are to observe the way the employee is currently doing the job and record it in terms which are consistent with the standards of performance. You might gather this data by checking: quality records, observing, counting data as the employee works, informally or formally interviewing the employee, reviewing complaints or lack of complaints by customers, or by any of the several other methods as discussed in class or in your text.

Do each of the four listed jobs. Identify the data in terms of measurements specified in "I" above. (Otherwise, be consistent!) Then, within parentheses following the identified current performance, list the method of gathering this data.

FOR PRACTICAL PURPOSES: If you are training a person to do something, and you have no way of measuring current performance, estimate from your experience what level a person in similar situations might achieve (perform at), or make an "educated" guess. Certainly, if you interview the person, you may learn something about his or her ability to perform at a particular level.

It is OK to state that the current performance is zero. The person simply may have no knowledge of this task. It is possible that a new employee will have no knowledge of any of the four jobs you identify. Simply state that fact in each item.

III. <u>IDENTIFY GAPS</u> - All you need to do in this item is to subtract the Current Performance "(II)" from the Desired Performance "(I)". If you have quantified your performance standards, this should be simple. NOTE: Make sure what you are going to train the person to do has a gap that is strong enough to mandate training. I get a little frustrated when someone says there is "no gap" and then proceed to announce that he/she is going to train the person to do that job. You wouldn't waste your time as a supervisor to train a person if there were no gap. The gap is the REASON or the identified NEED for training.

IV. <u>PRIORITIZE THE GAPS FOR ACTION</u>- Leave the identifying numbered or lettered notation in front of each job; this makes it easier to relate back to the desired and current performance. However re-arrange them in priority of need for training. Your first item here might be "B" or "D" rather than the normal "A-B-C-D" sequence. The highest item listed would be the highest priority for your training attention. In this model, make sure the first item you list is the item you plan to train someone to do. The wording should be identical to or can be interpreted as what you reported you were going to train the person to do.

V. <u>FORM STRATEGY TO CLOSE THE GAP(S)</u> - Now that you have identified and prioritized the performance gaps you need to determine the best strategy for closing them. This step helps you identify the strategy you are going to use to close these gaps. The use of the Problem Analysis flow chart enables you to take this performance discrepancy and determine whether or not this is a skill problem and if training is the solution.

In the process of developing a strategy to close the performance gaps take your performance discrepancy through a Performance Analysis flow chart (Mager has a good one). The Performance Analysis flow chart will help you identify whether the performance problem is skill related and therefore can be corrected with training. Problems not skill related can be corrected by changing the job, reward structure or the removal of obstacles to performance. Remember, not all performance problems are training problems. Many times, training money and efforts are wasted on problems that should not, or cannot, be solved with training

In this section, after analyze the performance problem,you simply state why you think training is the answer to item "--" (which is the first priority item in "IV"). You may say that additional training will be provided on other items where there is a gap identified, or state some general strategy that will follow this packet to help overcome other gaps. HOWEVER, DO NOT IDENTIFY MORE THAN ONE item to be the focus of training of this packet.

NOTE: The whole purpose of this part of the training packet is to justify and identify ONE area of training needed from among the several different responsibilities he or she might have on the job.

Follow the example on the attached sheet; take your problem from the questionnaire phase through the Problem Analysis phase.

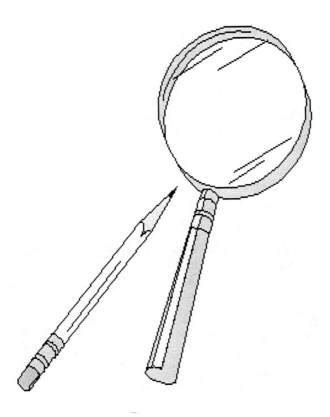

NEEDS ANALYSIS EXAMPLE

I. **IDENTIFIED DESIRED PERFORMANCE**
The molding machine operators should be able to . . .

    A.   Produce 55 molds per hour
    B.   Produce less than five percent scrap
    C.   Recognize the three major problems (sand too wet, bad cope and drag fits, machinery malfunctions), and troubleshoot the minor problems without shutting down the line
    D.   Shut down the line if a major problem occurs, and report it to the supervisor

II. **CURRENT PERFORMANCE**

    A.   Average production is 53 molds per hour (by past production records)
    B.   Scrap is currently averaging 9 percent (by past years' scrap record)
    C.   Forty percent of the line shutdowns could be corrected by the operator without shutting down the line (by supervisor questionnaire)
    D.   This is well done (by supervisor questionnaire)

III. **IDENTIFY GAPS**

    A.   Gap is two molds per hour
    B.   Gap is four percent scrap
    C.   Gap is thirty percent of the shutdowns
    D.   No gap exists

IV. **PRIORITIZE FOR ACTION**

    C.   Reduce unnecessary shutdowns
    B.   Reduce scrap
    A.   Produce two more molds per hour
    D.   No gap exists

V. **STRATEGY TO CLOSE GAPS**

I will develop a short training program on point III-C, along with giving some on- the-job assistance. Solving point C will help solve the problems in A and B. No action is needed for point D.

NEEDS ANALYSIS WORKSHEET

I. IDENTIFIED DESIRED PERFORMANCE (component performance)

The employee should be able to...

A. _____

B. _____

C. _____

D. _____

II. CURRENT PERFORMANCE

At present the employee is able to...

A. _____

B. _____

C. _____

D. _____

III. IDENTIFY GAPS (between desired and actual performance)

A. _____

B. _____

C. _____

D. _____

IV. PRIORTIZE GAPS FOR ACTION

A. _____

B. _____

C. _____

D. _____

V. STRATEGY TO CLOSE GAPS

_____

_____

_____

_____

PROBLEM ANALYSIS EXERCISE
(To be used with case study or video)

This exercise will give you the opportunity to apply the Performance Analysis process. As you view the following work situation, try to identify several different performance discrepancies. A performance discrepancy is when actual performance does not meet/fulfill the requirements of desired performance. After identifying the various performance discrepancies, you will work in groups to determine the most important discrepancy. Analyze that discrepancy using the problem analysis flow chart to determine the best solution to solve that problem. Answer the questions below.

What discrepancies in performance did you observe in this work situation?

1. _____

2. _____

3. _____

How would you describe what the ideal performance should be for the above performance discrepancies?

1. _____

2. _____

3. _____

Select what you think is the most important of the above performance problems. Using the Analysis Flow Chart analyze that problem to determine if the problem is a skill deficiency, or caused by a non-skill related problem. Also look at what you would do to solve it.

Is training a solution to this problem?

If training is not a solution then what would you do?

TRAINING PROPOSAL
(I think training is the solution--how do I sell it to the boss?)

The Training Proposal, like all proposals, is designed to ask permission to do a particular project. From your Needs analysis you have determined there is a problem and based on your problem analysis you feel training is the best solution. Now you have to sell your idea to management. Basically, the purpose of this proposal is to convince one's supervisor or manager that there is a problem and that the problem can be "fixed" in the way you describe. A complete and well-written proposal ensures that one's ideas are communicated clearly and increases the chance of gaining approval. A good proposal explains the problem, describes the proposed solution in detail, identifies costs, and justifies the expenditure of time, money and resources.

There is no one correct way to format a training proposal. However, as stated above, a good training proposal should contain specific information about the project. The exact content can be divided into areas for ease of understanding. **Also, review the reader's questions that we discussed in the Needs Analysis Proposal section.**

Typical format is a memo (block style) containing the following areas:

Heading:
From:
To:
Date:
Subject:

Background: The background section should contain a description of the problem (i.e., who is involved, the symptoms, and the causes), and what you have done to date regarding the problem. Address the performance discrepancy from your analysis. The purpose of this section is to demonstrate that there is a problem and that it is worth fixing.

Solution: It is often helpful to briefly and clearly describe the solution you are proposing. This will give your reader a "global" picture of what you are proposing to do. **Include in this section who the training is for, your broad training goals, a rough timetable for accomplishing this, and the expected results.**

Rationale: It is important to explain why you think this is the best solution. Two levels of justification are usually needed when we propose a project. First, you identify why the project needs to be done at all. This was discussed briefly in the "Background" section. However, you may want to summarize the reasons in this section as well. Second, you must convince your supervisor that the proposed solution is the best solution. Explain why the project should be done in the way you have proposed. This is also a good time to explain what will happen if there is no training program.

Budget: This is a basic look at what resources will be needed to put this together. Consider your own situation as if you were in a company; for example, if you already have a video camera then you won't need to rent one, etc. Consider the budgeting issues discussed on the next two pages.

BUDGETING FOR TRAINING
(What is this going to cost?)

A critical aspect of any training program is "What will it cost?" Cost considerations cover the whole spectrum, from initial analysis to the number of people who will be trained and/or number of sessions. With the large variety of training equipment available, training technology must also be considered ("It is great but is it affordable?"). The following format will take you through some considerations regarding budgeting.

FORMAT:

Introduction: Describe briefly what, how and where the training session will be. What is its purpose? Tell how many sessions per year, and how many people will be in each session.

Developmental Costs: Itemize material and staff costs which will be incurred in developing the training unit.

   a. Planning: How much will you charge for developing your unit? HINT: Most trainers are NOT charity workers. Your time is worth something!

   b. Staff: Did you use a secretary, photographer, A/V resource person?

   c. Materials: Did you rent or buy any equipment? Did you use a copy service for printing handouts?

TOTAL the developmental costs (remember, these are costs incurred only during the development of your unit).

Operational Costs: Itemize daily costs incurred during the actual training service (or that you predict will be spent). These may include the conference leaders or trainer's salary (that could be you!), refreshments (if the company is paying), lodging and travel costs per trainee, facilities rental, salaries of employees being trained, materials for distribution (do not repeat those charged already against developmental costs), any rentals, etc.

   TOTAL the operational costs (remember, these are the specific costs incurred during the actual training).

Instructional Cost Index: Amortize developmental costs (decide how many sessions you will have in a year, then divide developmental costs by that number). Add operational costs of the actual training session.

   TOTAL I.C.I. (Instructional Cost Index) is determined when you divide the above total (previous line) by the number of trainees attending each session.

EXAMPLE

Introduction: The purpose of this training is to eliminate unnecessary time-consuming expensive interruptions of a physician's time. This can be done by proper screening of telephone calls. The training is done with discussion and on-the-job techniques. Most of the training is done in the medical office reception area. A different person will be trained in each of six sessions per year.

Developmental Costs:

Trainer's time to develop program 20 hours @ $40.00 =	$800.00
Physician's time for his assistance 1 hour @ $100.00 =	100.00
Secretary's time to type 7 hours @ $7.00 =	49.00
Paper and supplies for developing program	25.00
TOTAL	$974.00

Operational Costs:

Refreshments	$ 15.00
Trainee wages (1 person x $7 per hour for 6 hours)	42.00
Trainer salary (1 x $40 per hour for 6 hours)	240.00
Materials for distribution	15.00
TOTAL	$312.00

Instructional Cost Index:

Developmental cost $974 divided by six sessions =	$162.33
Add operational costs	$312.00
TOTAL	$474.33
Divided by number to be trained in a session (474.33 / 1) =	$474.33 (I.C.I.)

34

TRAINING PROPOSAL WORKSHEET

From: (Your Names)
To: Mr. Krug, Manager
Date: June 3, 1993
Re: Training proposal for _____

(Background) _____

_____

_____

_____

(Solution) _____

_____

_____

_____

(Rationale) _____

_____

_____

_____

Budget:

Video Camera	$_____	
Supplies	$_____	
Facilities	$_____	
Personnel	$_____	
Total	$_____	

Do not include the paragraph titles such as (Background).

LEARNER ANALYSIS
(Who is this person I am trying to train?)

Before developing the learning activities and materials, you should describe the learners for whom you are designing the packet. Learners differ in aptitude, preference for type of learning, motivation, and experience. This variance will affect your instructional strategies, delivery systems, and media selection. You need to determine what will work best for a particular learner with particular characteristics under certain conditions with specific desired outcomes.

When doing a learner assessment consider the following three factors:

- Situation-related factors:
    - What are the possible relationships between the performance problem and the learner?
    - Does the performance problem itself suggest unique characteristics of the learner?
    - Will their characteristics remain the same over time?
- Decision-related factors:
    - Who makes the decision about which people will participate in instruction?
- Learner-related factors:
    - Stem from the learners themselves. Prerequisite knowledge, skills, and attitudes.

Recent studies have determined that different generations perceive and react to training situations differently. This difference needs to be considered when developing training whether or not the learners are all of one generation or combination of generations. The following is a summary of characteristics of the different generations: (The Generation Gaps in the Classroom, Training Magazine, November 1999, by Zemke, Raines and Filipczak)

- Veterans (1922-1943)
    - Prefers a learning environment that is stable, orderly and risk free.
    - They are conformers, appreciate logic, and are disciplined.
    - They respect authority – not likely to disagree with you.
    - They don't like to be put on the spot.

- Baby Boomers (1943-1960)
    - Like interaction and non-authoritarian style of instruction.
    - They are dedicated learners
    - They like a trainer who treats them as equals.
    - Are motivated to learn if it gives them a new way to win or get ahead.
    - They dislike role-playing.
    - Intellectually they may know things but these do not always translate into skills.

- The Generation X-ers (1961-1980)
    - Prefer self-directed learning environment
    - Believe that if the job gets done it does not matter how or when
    - They don't like structure
    - They like formats that include CR-ROM, videos, electronic support systems
    - They don't read as much as older or younger generations
    - Like visual stimulation

36

- The Generation Next (1980-Present)
  - Prefer a learning environment that combines team and technology.
  - Like to be given a task
  - Like training materials that entertain them
  - Are readers
  - Technology is natural to them
  - If technology is not used then trainer's don't know their stuff
  - They want skills that will make them more marketable and/or the job less stressful

Learner Analysis Assignment:

List in detail everything you know about the learner that is relevant to the content or skills you plan to teach. Your list might include such variables as: prior knowledge, familiarity with content to be learned, and/or degree of motivation. This kind of information will govern your approach to the learner in style, vocabulary level, and amount of repetition and reinforcement. There are TWO types of information you will need to specify about your students. The <u>first</u> is general <u>learner characteristics</u>, factors that describe the learner. The second category is <u>specific entry behavior</u> (or what the learners are expected to be able to do <u>before</u> beginning the training program). The Learner Analysis contains four (4) parts as described below.

I. LEARNER CHARACTERISTICS

Under the heading of Learner Characteristics, you should list any factor(s) that may affect student learning of the material(s) to be presented. These characteristics tend to be stable and do not change over a short period of time.

SOME OF THE CHARACTERISTICS MIGHT BE . . .

--age/grade level
--attention span
--physical/mental handicaps
--level of motivation
--intelligence
--personality characteristics
--verbal ability
--learning style

--socio-economic status
--emotional maturity
--dexterity for motor tasks
--technical vocabulary
--reading ability
--mathematical ability
--special interests
    --visual or verbal orientation

You do not need to address all of these, just those that might be pertinent to the area or person being trained. If age is not a factor then don't list it. However, there are areas where it certainly <u>does</u> make a difference. **Avoid areas such as race, sex, and religion to preclude the appearance of discrimination**

37

II. SPECIFIC ENTRY BEHAVIOR (Prerequisites!!)

Entry behavior is the level of ability and competence at which the learner begins instruction. Identify those behaviors or skills the learner MUST already possess in order to learn. This could include knowledge, attitudes, or skills which are necessary before the person can learn what you are teaching. The purpose of the instruction is to advance the learners from where they are (ENTRY BEHAVIOR) to where you would like the learners to be (TERMINAL BEHAVIOR).

FORMULA:
> Entry Behavior + Instruction + Motivation = Terminal Behavior (Competency)

Obviously it is necessary to clearly specify the skills and knowledge that the learners must possess if they are to succeed. Vague, broad, "shotgun" descriptions lack specificity, and are of little or no value to the learners. You might want to state (1) what previous training (knowledge) the learners should have, (2) what tests they must have passed, and even (3) what scores they must have attained. For a technical typist to be able to participate in an advanced program might require the following entry behavior: "The ability to type 60 words per minute with 90 percent accuracy in a five-minute timed test."

In short, unless you can be specific about the learner's needed competencies in measurable terms, you will not know where to begin with your training. Often, a statement such as, "There are no prerequisites for this training" misleads students into thinking they can succeed, when in reality, they may fail to achieve because of insufficient entry behavior data. Almost all instruction will have prerequisite skills, such as the ability to read at a certain level, or the ability to comprehend the spoken English language. Many times, these skills prerequisites are taken for granted. For this assignment, practice identifying the prerequisites, even to the extent of identifying an assumption.

Another common error is to state in the entry behavior that the learners should have "completed a course in welding." While they may have taken a course, they may not have achieved the skills (or learning objectives) of that course. Thus, they may have taken a course in welding, but not achieved the ability to actually perform a smooth bead, or to have met some other "criterion referenced standard".

It is highly recommended that you state the entry behavior in the same format as the objectives. Let's look at the following entry behavior requirement for trainees with the following general objective:

> "The student will need to be able to translate and interpret into English a minimum
> of 80 percent of conversational Spanish on a bi-lingual test before entering the
> training of a crisis center counselor with the Dade County Crisis Control Center."

In determining the entry behavior you ask: "What must the trainee be able to do before beginning the training?"

List only learner competencies that have direct relevance to the instructional situation. Normally, those competencies that are indirectly related can be assumed and not spelled out in detail. If you have difficulty finding any learner competencies at all, then spell out some of the assumed competencies. Of course, the trainee must be able to read the instruction. You should verify that the student can read at the level at which the instruction is written.

38

III.   GOAL STATEMENT

When looking at the Learner Analysis, it sometimes makes sense to look once again at the general idea of what you want to accomplish with this training. "What do I want to accomplish with this training?" focuses on the difference between the entry behavior, and what WILL BE, or what the trainee will have mastered (terminal behavior) as a result of your training.

This statement is not intended to be objectives with performance and criteria terms. It does not necessarily need to look like the needs analysis statement on broad goals.

IV.   PURPOSE STATEMENT

The purpose statement should answer the question "Why do I want to accomplish this training?" It should focus on the reasons why the training is important.

39

EXAMPLE

LEARNER ANALYSIS

I. LEARNER CHARACTERISTICS: A list of learner characteristics (used to guide the development of your training packet for training managers who are studying the concept of motivation) might contain the following:

The typical person being trained will be . . .

1. Male or female age 28-45
2. A high school education
3. A 10-year employee with the company, with at least five years experience in other areas of the foundry
4. Average to below-average in intelligence
5. Strong in mechanical knowledge and skills
6. A union member with strong a belief in doing the job according to the union contract
7. Familiar with the flow of materials throughout the foundry

II. ENTRY BEHAVIOR

Before training, the typical person should be able to . . .

1. Set cores of all types correctly, at a 99 percent efficiency rate
2. Operate the sand conditioner to company specifications
3. Lift 50 pounds using the proper safe lifting techniques
4. Communicate technical information to the supervisor in technical terms

III. GOAL STATEMENT

With this training program, the worker can reduce the amount of scrap that is due to poor molding to no more than five percent of the total number of castings.

IV. PURPOSE STATEMENT

To reduce the amount of scrap in order to increase productivity and decrease cost. Eliminating the cost of re-melted scrap, wasted cores, and extra labor for sorting and casting can save money.

40

LEARNER ANALYSIS WORKSHEET

LEARNER ANALYSIS

I.   Learner Characteristics:

The typical person being trained will be...

1._____
2._____
3._____
4._____
5._____

II.   Entry Behavior:

Before training, the typical person should be able to...

1._____
2._____
3._____
4._____
5._____

III. Goal Statement (What?):

_____

_____

_____

_____

IV.   Purpose Statement (Why?):

_____

_____

_____

_____

41

TASK ANALYSIS
(What is involved in doing this job?)

A Capture of Component Performance

The Task Analysis involves the systematic process of identifying specific tasks to be trained, and a detailed analysis of each in terms of frequency, difficulty and importance. A Task Analysis sequences and describes observable, measurable behaviors involved in the performance of a task/job. It is the process of breaking down the task, or job, into functional behavioral units (Wall, Haught, & Dower, 1982: Spaid, 1986). When conducting a task analysis, specify the exact behaviors your learner must exhibit to perform the task. When determining how much detail should be used in breaking down the task consider the learner. Learners with fewer prerequisite skills will need more detailed steps than more experienced learners.

I. GENERAL FACTORS ABOUT A TASK ANALYSIS (TA):

The information obtained for a TA can be used as the foundation for:

a. Developing instructional objectives,
b. Sequencing instructional content,
c. Identifying and selecting appropriate instructional media,
d. Designing performance evaluation tools,
e. Identifying and selecting appropriate instructional methods and strategies

A Task Analysis consists of five parts:

1. What initiates this action?
2. The tasks involved
3. The steps involved in this task
4. The knowledge needed to perform the steps in this task
5. What signals that the task is complete?

A thorough Task Analysis will accomplish the following:

a. Explain what a "good" job is
b. Help the supervisor understand the workflow; so better ways can be created to do the job
c. Help in write training objectives
d. Help facilitate better training
e. Identify performance standards to be used in performance appraisal
f. Help evaluate the job for upgrading or pay increases

Types of questions addressed in a Task Analysis

- How difficult or complex is the task?
- What behaviors are used in the performance of the job?
- How frequently is the task performed?
- How critical is the task to the performance of the job?
- To what degree is the task performed individually, or is part of a set of collective tasks?
- If a subset of set of collective tasks, what is the relationship between the various tasks?
- What is the consequence if the task is performed incorrectly or is not performed at all?
- To what extent can the task be trained on the job?
- What level of task proficiency is expected following training?

42

II. <u>HOW TO START A TASK ANALYSIS</u>

    a. Observe employees doing the job, and analyze workflow

    b. Read the manual of operation describing the work/job, if available

    c. Do the job yourself

    d. Ask (interview) the employee currently doing the job

III. <u>FORMAT</u>

    a. Divide the job into as many general categories as needed. Each category is called an OPERATION;

    b. List STEPS for each operation, and then...

    c. List KEY POINTS (knowledge) for each step. These are specific points which elaborate on the procedures for completing the steps.

See example on following page.

43

A Task Analysis Case Study: Carter Cleaning Company (The New Training Program)

At the present time Carter Cleaning Centers have no formal 0prientation or training policies or procedures, and Jennifer believes this is one reason why the standards that she and her father would like employees to adhere to are generally not followed.

Several examples can illustrate this. In dealing with the customers at the front counters the Carters would prefer that certain practices and procedures be used. For example, all customers should be greeted with what Jack refers to as a "big hello". Any garments they drop off should immediately be inspected for any damage or unusual stains so these can be brought to the customer's attention, lest the customer later return to pick up the garment and erroneously blame the store for the damage or the unusual stain. The garments are then supposed to be immediately placed together in a nylon sack to separate them from other customers' garments. The ticket also has to be carefully written up with the customer's name telephone number, and the date precisely and clearly noted on all copies. The counter person is also supposed to take the opportunity to try to sell the customer some additional services, such as waterproofing, if a raincoat has been dropped off, or simply notifying the customer that "you know now that people are doing their spring cleaning, we're having a special on drapery cleaning all this month." Finally as the customer leaves, the counterperson is supposed to make some courteous comments like "Have a nice day" or "Drive safely." Each of the other jobs in the stores – pressing, cleaning and spotting, periodically maintaining the coin laundry equipment, and so forth – similarly contain certain steps, procedures, and most important, standards which the Carters would prefer to see adhered to.

The company has also had other problems, Jennifer feels, because of a lack of adequate employee training and orientation. For example, two new employees became very upset last month when they discovered that they were not paid at the end of the week, on Friday, but instead were paid (as are all Carter employees) on the following Tuesday. The Carters use the extra two day in part to give them time to obtain everyone's hours and compute their pay. the other reason they do it, according to jack, is that "frankly, when we stay a few days behind in paying employees it helps to ensure that they at least give us a few days notice before quitting on us. While we are certainly obligated to pay them anything they earn, we find that psychologically they seem to be less likely to just walk out on us Friday evening and not show up Monday morning if they still haven't gotten their pay from the previous week. This way they at least give us a few day's notice so we can find a replacement."

Other matters that could be covered during an orientation include company policy regarding paid holidays, lateness and absences, health and hospitalization benefits (there are none, other than worker's compensation) and general matters like maintaining a clean and sage work area, personal appearance and cleanliness, filling in time sheets, personal telephone calls and mail, company policies regarding matters like substance abuse, and eating or smoking on the job.

Jennifer believes that implementing orientation and training programs would help to ensure that employees know how to do their jobs the right was. And she and her father further believe that it is only when employees understand the right way to do their jobs that there is any hope that their jobs will in fact be accomplished the way the Carters want them to be accomplished.

Questions:
1. Specifically what should the Carters cover in their new employee orientation program and how should they cover this information?
2. Should Jennifer do a task analysis for the counter person's job and is so what, roughly speaking, would the completed, filled-in form look like?
3. Which specific training techniques should she use to train her pressers, her cleaner-spotters, her managers, and her counter people, and why?

Human Resource Management. Sixth Edition, Gary Dessler, Prentice hall. 1994

44

Task Analysis Example: **Instructional Guide to Using Video Equipment**

When initiated: When video equipment is being used.

OPERATIONS	STEPS	KNOWLEDGE KEY POINTS
1. Check and see if all of the necessary video equipment is present.	1.Make sure that you have back-up videotape. 2.Make sure that you have back up charged batteries.	Battery life lasts two hours. Extra tapes needed because of emergencies and tape damage.
2. Insert battery into battery pack (back of camera)	1.Make sure power switch is on. 2.Press DMS button (side of camera) to check battery life. 3. Look into viewfinder in upper left had corner there will be E---F. 4. Look to make sure there are four dotted lines between the E and F.	If you do not have all four lines showing, you need to recharge battery or get new battery.
3. Insert cassette into side of machine.	1. Press eject button to open door. 2. Insert cassette with window side facing cassette door and arrow on cassette is facing down. 3. Close camera door.	If tape is not in the machine correctly then recording will not take place.
4. Adjust control switches.	1. Make sure the S-VHS selector (left side of camera) is switched to S-VHC. 2. Make sure tape speed selector (left side of camera) is set on SLP. 3. Make sure the VCR/camera switch (top of camera) is on camera.	If S-VHS is not set then camera will operate as VHS. Camera produces better video when on SLP. If button is not slid to camera recording will not take place.
5. Adjust viewfinder and eyepiece.	1. Slide viewfinder out from camera into a comfortable position for the camera operator.	The viewfinder must be comfortable for the operator or shots will be distorted.
6. Prepare to record video.	1. Set the focus switch (near the lens of camera) to Auto Focus. 2. Make sure you have appropriate shot. 3. Press record button (right by hand holder). 4. After completion of shot push pause button (same as record button) to stop recording. 5. If camera goes to standby as a result of being on pause for more than 5 minutes, push standby button (top of camera).	You must see the full range through the viewfinder. When camera is in Auto Focus the images produced will be clearer. Standby goes into effect in order to conserve battery power.
7. Completion of recording	1. Turn power off first. 2. Eject the battery. 3. Eject the tape cassette. 4. Pack up equipment.	Always make sure power is off when ejecting battery of damage may occur. Pack up equipment.

When complete: When tape has been successfully shot.

45

TASK ANALYSIS EXAMPLE FOLLOWS:

TASK ANALYSIS: receptionist at doctor's office.

When initiated: When a patient calls.

OPERATIONS	STEPS	KNOWLEDGE/ KEY POINTS
I. Answer the phone.	1. Lift receiver off hook and speak into mouthpiece. 2. Respond: "Good Morning, Dr. Jones' office," etc.	Keep a cheerful voice. Be empathetic; the caller may be sick and needing help.
II. Find out purpose of the call/caller.	1. If information is volunteered, listen. 2. If information is not volunteered, tell caller the doctor is with a patient and ask what you can do to help the caller to then listen.	Be sure to get pencils and paper ready to record information. Remember almost all patients would prefer to talk to the doctor.
III. Mentally determine if call meets doctor's guidelines on whether to interrupt or transfer calls to him.	1. Check guideline list 2. Pull patient's chart and read most recent notations.	Remember: unnecessary interruptions lengthen the workday for the staff.
IV. Make every effort to satisfy the caller's inquiry without interrupting the doctor or upsetting the patient.	1. Offer another source of information if possible. 2. Offer information which you can ethically give. 3. Make appointment for patient to see doctor. 4. Take request for prescriptions. 5. Suggest alternative solutions- emergency room or nurse or medication. 6. Take phone number for doctor to return call if he is busy now.	Remember: you are NOT the physician, so don't prescribe treatment.
V. If all else fails or if best judgment determines the doctor should be called, do with confidence!		
VI. Terminate phone call in a pleasant manner.	1. Record all pertinent information on patient's chart.	

When complete: When phone call ends and information is recorded.

46

TASK ANALYSIS WORKSHEET

Task Title: _____

When initiated: _____

OPERATIONS	STEPS	KNOWLEDGE/ KEY POINTS
I._____ _____ _____ _____ _____	1._____ 2._____ 3._____ _____	_____ _____ _____ _____
II._____ _____ _____ _____ _____	1._____ 2._____ 3._____ _____	_____ _____ _____ _____
III._____ _____ _____ _____ _____	1._____ 2._____ 3._____ _____	_____ _____ _____ _____
IV._____ _____ _____ _____	1._____ 2._____ 3._____ _____	_____ _____ _____ _____
V. _____ _____ _____ _____	1._____ 2._____ 3._____ _____	_____ _____ _____ _____
VI._____ _____ _____ _____	1._____ 2._____ 3._____ _____	_____ _____ _____ _____

When complete:_____

47

LEARNING OBJECTIVES
(How do I put the content of the Task Analysis into an instructional format?)

The development of clear concise learning objectives is critical to the successful development and delivery of any training program. Learning objectives do the following things:
- Aids in communicating material to the learner
- Demonstrates desired quality
- Focuses the learner on what they need to know
- Used for media, instructional methods, and instructional strategy selection
- Used to set the criteria for evaluation
- Provides a road map for learning

In the Task Analysis we determined the operations, steps, and knowledge (capture of competent performance) needed to accomplish a given task or job. We now need to put those items into the learning objective format to clarify what we are trying to teach. Your learning objectives will be the basis for the rest of your packet. Once you write and analyze the objectives, you will sequence them, and then design your performance evaluation, instructional strategy, and rough draft (lesson plan) according to the objectives.

In training, objectives are written in terms of performance (behavior) that are detailed descriptions of what the trainee will be able to accomplish during and following training. There are different formats for writing objectives, but we will concentrate on the PCC method.

PCC- METHOD OF WRITING OBJECTIVES

(P) Performance: The *performance* component describes, "What a learner will be doing when demonstrating mastery of the objective". The skill or action that the trainee is to perform. The performance is defined by using an action verb that describes the desired skill or action i.e. to list, to accept, to repair, depending on the domain of learning to which you are training.

(C) Criterion: The *criterion* component describes, "How well the learner must perform in order to be considered acceptable". How will the accomplishment of this skill, behavior, or attitude be measured, (standard or degree). It is important to consider the method of evaluation as well as the standard of evaluation.

(C) Condition: The *condition* component "describes the important condition under which the performance is to occur. Under what circumstances or conditions this action will take place. In defining the condition you must consider the action as well as the trainee. It is important to identify the cue or stimulus that initiates this action and the framework under which this action takes place.

Another way to write effective learning objectives is to write them so that they include the following items:

(A) Audience (Learner) – Who performs the task
(B) Behavior (Skill or Action) – Begins with a measurable verb and demonstrates what the leaner does to show mastery.
(C) Conditions (What circumstances) – Describes the important conditions (if any) under which the performance is to occur. This may include tools or even environmental conditions
(D) Degree (Measurement) – How well the learner must perform to be considered acceptable? Normally listed in terms of Speed, Quantity, Quality, Time Limit

48

Learning objectives are classified into different levels (domains) in order to establish how in-depth the material must be taught to and therefore learned by the learners. Objectives are classified into three different domains of learning; Cognitive (knowledge and information), Psychomotor (doing or physical skills), and Affective (attitudes and feelings).

When planning instruction, it is important to consider the different domains of learning and the levels within each of the different domains. **The domain of learning as well as the level of learning is dependent upon the material being presented, the learner being taught, and the degree of skill you are trying to achieve.** The selection of teaching methods, materials, and evaluation techniques is directly tied to the domain and level of learning.

LEARNING DOMAINS AND LEVELS OF LEARNING
(What level of learning is required?)

COGNITIVE DOMAIN (Knowledge, Information, Intellectual Learning)

Bloom (1956) developed a six level taxonomy which he saw as hierarchical: that is, learning builds by exposure to content at the lower level and becomes more complex as you move up the taxonomy. The levels for lowest to highest are:

KNOWLEDGE (simplest learning) - includes recognition, remembering, and recall of basic facts but does not imply understanding of content.
Example: The learner will be able to label the parts of the ear on a drawing.

COMPREHENSION (knowing what a message means) - The learner not only knows but can demonstrate comprehension of information.
Example: The learner will be able to explain the procedure for performing a sales account search using the Lotus 1-2-3 program.

APPLICATION (demonstration and/or using what was previously learned) - The use of rules, principles, and basic knowledge in the solving of problems. Trainee doing the actual application of learned knowledge in a simulation or on the job.
Example: The learner will be able to write an objective that includes the key elements of objectives.

ANALYSIS (disassembling a whole into parts) - Learners are able to take apart the learned material, understand the relationship between ideas, and then be able to compare and contrast the parts.
Example: The learner will observe two different troubleshooting techniques for the same problem and be able to compare and contrast the strategies used to solve the problem.

SYNTHESIS (assembling w whole from parts) - The learner can put together information, concepts or positions from a variety of sources into one product.
Example: The learner will prepare a sales proposal to be given to a customer based upon the latest production schedule and price lists.

EVALUATION (assessing the value of ideas, things, and so on) - Includes judgments of quality based on established criteria, in an objective evaluation based on knowledge of what should be involved in some piece of work.
Example: The learner will be able to evaluate the strengths and limitations of two design proposals, compare them, and be able to justify their decision as to which is best.

49

AFFECTIVE DOMAIN (Attitude and Feelings)

Has five levels of learning dealing with the learning of attitudes, beliefs, and awareness.

RECEIVING - (Paying attention) The learner simply is aware of and willing to receive a value, belief or attitude.

RESPONDING - (Participating) The learner responds to the presentation of values in either a positive or negative manner.

VALUING - (Accepting values/beliefs) The learner shows consistency and commitment to beliefs, values, and attitudes.

ORGANIZATION - (Developing/acquiring a new value system) The learner organizes values, beliefs, and attitudes into a system, determines the interrelationships among them, and selects the strongest ones.

CHARACTERIZATION - (Adopting a new way of life or outlook)The learner has adopted a belief or value system.

PSYCHOMOTOR (Skills, Muscle coordination)

In this domain there are seven levels dealing with learning new skills and the ability to perform them. Some authors relate levels in this domain to the lowest levels in Bloom's taxonomy for the cognitive domain (knowledge, comprehension, application).

PERCEPTION - (Observing behaviors involved in a task) Includes awareness of objects or cues and the association of these cues with the task to be performed.

SET - (Getting ready to perform) Readiness for a particular action, like knowing the proper stance for lifting a heavy object.

GUIDED RESPONSE - (Performing a task with assistance) performing a specific skill that will become the component of a more complex skill.

MECHANISM - (Acting without assistance) Behavior learned or modeled becomes a habit, and learner is proficient at carrying it out.

COMPLEX OVERT RESPONSE - (Performing automatically with facility/habitually) Actions are performed without hesitation, or automatically.

ADAPTATION - Learner is able to adapt motor activities to meet unanticipated demands of the situation.

ORIGINATION - The ability to create new motor actions based on previously developed skills.

The use of a taxonomy in the psychomotor and affective domains serves the same purpose as it does in the cognitive domain. The awareness of the stages of learning for a particular skill or attitude is important in ensuring that instruction includes the necessary prerequisite behaviors.

50

LEARNING OBJECTIVES EXERCISE

Instructions: For each of the following statements, identify if the statement is a good or bad behavioral objective. If bad, what is missing and how would you change it?

1. Given a hammer, wood, nails, and a blueprint, the student will construct a birdhouse so that all measurements are within blueprint tolerances.

2. The student will know how to safely lift heavy objects.

3. Given a procedure sheet and a packing machine, the student will clean the machine with at least 15 of 18 steps done correctly.

4. Given a written quiz, the student will know the major parts of the human body with at least 85% accuracy.

5. Given a list of 35 chemical elements, recall and write the valences of at least 30.

6. The student will develop an appreciation for safety.

7. Given a widget kit and references, the learner will assemble the widget so that it functions as designed.

8. Given a computer, cleaning materials, and a procedure sheet, the trainee must be able to clean the computer. This objective is satisfied if the student completes 90% of the steps correctly.

ASSIGNMENT GUIDELINES

Format: **First write a Training Goal (overall objective).** This can come from your goal statement as stated in the Learner Analysis. **Then write a minimum of one learning objective for each major point of your Task Analysis.**

You should write six to 10 objectives. If the major point has several sub-points, give serious thought to writing additional objectives. On the other hand, if the task analysis has more than 10 major points, you may combine or omit some of the content to reduce the objectives to a more workable level.

Write your objectives in the PCC format. (Performance, Criterion, Condition).

Now **classify each of the objectives into the proper domain** - cognitive, psychomotor, and affective. (If it is cognitive, specify the level also: knowledge, comprehension, application, analysis, synthesis, and evaluation.). This will help you when selecting your instructional methods.

51

<u>EXAMPLES</u> (from three different projects):

Given gear ratios, the trainee will install the proper gears inside the gearbox. The trainee will do this within 20 minutes, for five different gear ratios, correctly 98 percent of the time. (Psychomotor)

Given an article of clothing, the employee should be able to indicate the proper   rack or stand where it should be placed with 90 percent accuracy. (Cognitive knowledge)

Given $368.00 in mixed bills, the trainee should be able to count it aloud using the unit system. This should be done in less than 20 seconds with 100 percent accuracy. (Psychomotor, Cognitive knowledge)

Job Aid for Writing Learning Objectives

Action Verb _____

Audience (Learner)_____

Behavior (Skill or Action) _____

Conditions (What circumstances?)_____

Degree (Measurement) _____

Time (Limit) _____

A _____

A _____

B _____

C _____

D _____

T _____

52

Objective writing practice area: You are training United Vans Lines truck drivers on how to plan delivery of furniture from Lafayette, Indiana to Sheboygan, Wisconsin. Delivery is expected in 5 days. Write the following:

Write an overall training goal that you hope to accomplish with your training program.

_____

_____

_____

_____

Write three learning objectives that are necessary for the accomplishment of your training goal.

1. _____

_____

_____

_____

2. _____

_____

_____

_____

3._____

_____

_____

_____

8th Nov.
15th Nov.
29th Nov.

53

LEARNER OJECTIVES WORKSHEET

Training Goal: _____

_____

Learner Objectives:

1. _____

_____

_____(Domain:_____)

2. _____

_____

_____(Domain:_____)

3. _____

_____

_____(Domain:_____)

4. _____

_____

_____(Domain:_____)

5. _____

_____

_____(Domain:_____)

6. _____

_____

_____(Domain:_____)

7. _____

_____

_____(Domain:_____)

8. _____

_____

_____(Domain:_____)

PERFORMANCE TERMS FOR WRITING OBJECTIVES

The below performance terms will help your objectives to clearly state the desired level of learning you intend to take the learner to. The clearer the learner is as to how in-depth they need to know the material the easier your job is to get them there.

AFFECTIVE

Attitudes:

Accepts	Adopts	Advocates	Attends	Likes
Loves	Objects	Offers	Persists	Promotes
Volunteers	Watches	Seeks	Rejects	Enjoys
Chooses				

COGNITIVE

Knowledge

Defines	Lists
Names	Gives
Offers	Tells
Writes	Indicates
Identifies	Holds
Designates	Notes

Comprehension

Demonstrates	Explains
Defines (in own words)	
Interprets	Tells
Shows	Restates
Rephrases	Illustrates

Application

Uses	Applies
Generates	Relates
Integrates	Pictures

Analysis

Breaks down	Dissects
Disassembles	Divides
Investigates	Examines
Simplifies	Contrasts
Distinguishes	

Synthesis

Blends	Builds
Combines	Creates
Develops	Fashions
Reorganizes	Designs
Systematizes	Modifies

Evaluation

Appraises	Assesses
Calculates value of	
Grades	Ranks
Rates	Decides
Judges	Validates

Not acceptable

Appreciate
Know
Recognize
Understand

55

PERFORMANCE EVALUATION/TESTING
(How and why should I measure learning?)

Evaluation is the foundation of the training and development process. It is the means by which we make sure that we are actually teaching what should be taught and are doing so effectively. We look at evaluation from two different but related viewpoints: evaluating whether or not trainees learned (summative evaluation), and evaluating whether we were effective in our instructional process (formative evaluation).

CATEGORIES OF INSTRUCTIONAL EVALUATION

FORMATIVE EVALUATION: An ongoing assessment carried out throughout the training. Used to determine progress and/or weakness in *the instructional process* both before and during its implementation.

During development, ask:
> Why is this instruction being developed?
> What instructional objectives should be developed?
> What types of activities are needed?

While teaching, ask:
> Am I maintaining the original instructional purpose?
> Is the instruction suitable for the learner's needs?
> Are the learners responding as expected?
> Are they learning?

After the lesson or course is over, ask:
> Did the learners learn and did I instruct properly?

Formative evaluation tools include pretests, oral questioning, performance quizzes, and instructional activities. Also included can be questionnaires, observations, class participation, and oral presentations.

SUMMATIVE EVALUATION: Measures the degree to which the lesson or course has met its intended goal and whether or not your learners can actually perform the requirements of the job. Summative evaluation is important in the determination of the return on investment. Examples of summative measures are overall course reviews, and overall assessments of personnel job readiness over specific periods of time.

Evaluation tools include:

Multiple-choice tests	True false tests
Matching tests	Fill in the blank tests
Short answer tests	Essay tests
Performance tests	

56

Reviewing your test items: Regardless of the type or the format, as you review your evaluation tool, ask yourself the following questions:

*Does the item truly measure what I am trying to measure?

*Will the intent of the item be clear to someone reading it for the first time?

*Do my learners have all the information they need to answer the item?

*Is the wording as clear and concise as possible? If not, can the item be revised?

*Does the stem contain just one central theme?

*Are the distracters plausible, appropriate, and correct and do they make grammatical sense?

Why should you evaluate the results of your training? As a supervisor, you will be able to:

1. Determine if the trainees are achieving the objectives
2. Justify to upper management the money spent on training
3. Help motivate the trainees
4. Help revise and improve the training
5. Help market future training programs
6. Provide a learning experience for the trainees
7. Determine a cost/benefit analysis

Evaluation tools:

Questionnaires, interviews, paper/pencil tests, observations of job performances, role playing, case studies, group discussions, oral quizzes, computer tests, simulations/games, planned demonstrations by trainees, and performance records.

Levels of evaluation:

I   **Reaction:**   What did participants say about the program?

II   **Learning:**   What knowledge, skill, and/or attitudes were learned?

III **Behavior:**   Did the training actually bring about a change in behavior?

IV   **Results:**   Did the training pay off (return on investment)?

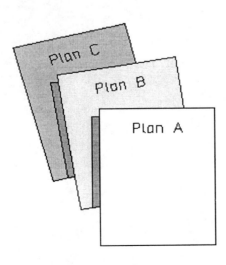

ASSIGNMENT GUIDELINES

Part I

Format: Contains three important parts.

> List the first objective in <u>summary form</u>.
> List the method you will use to evaluate the trainee on this objective.
> Name the level of evaluation you will be using.

Follow this format for each objective.

EXAMPLE I

Objective 1: Turn on the molding machine and run 10 consecutive molds with no more than one defective mold.

Testing: Planned demonstration by employee. This can be done during normal operating hours with a minimum of disruption.

Level: Behavior; learning.

EXAMPLE II

Objective 2: Given the name of a clothes rack or stand, explain the location and the rationale.

Testing: Oral quiz by supervisor.

Level: Learning.

Part II

Once the evaluation method and level are determined for each objective, then develop an evaluation tool that will be given to the trainees during and/or upon completion of training. This evaluation tool will be used to determine whether or not the trainee has learned the material. Follow Chapter 5 in your text on how to write evaluation questions.

1. Write at least two evaluation questions for each objective that will measure the trainee's accomplishment of that objective. Use one of the following formats: true/false, multiple choices, fill in the blank, oral or essay.

2. Your total evaluation should contain at least 15 questions and have at least one of each of the question formats in #1 above.

3. Develop and include an answer key that will go with this evaluation in the trainer's manual. The examination without answers will go in the trainee's manual.

4. Use a variety of question types, the textbook will help you determine which type of question to use in each situation. See some examples next page.

58

Examples:

What is the main utensil used for cleaning windows in preparation for tint application?

     a. putty knife
     b. razor knife
     c. Exacto knife
     d. ice scraper

It is important to leave the glass free of _____ and _____.

T/F: Tint should be cut to the exact shape of the glass.

Briefly describe the process of separating the tint from the cellophane backing.

List the steps involved in applying tint to a window.

Optional Evaluation Method: (Criterion referenced observation)

Depending on what you are training, evaluation can sometimes be more accurately done by observation during trainee demonstration of the learned procedure (like when you took your driver's license check ride). If this is the best way then carefully set up a simulation with observable standards so that the trainee can be evaluated fairly. If this is the better method of evaluation then follow the directions below.

a. Develop a simulation with observable standards.

b. Develop a checklist that identifies the steps to be accomplished and the standards to which they are to be accomplished.

c. The checklist must contain at least 15 items and must define the skill and the standard of accomplishment.

d. Include detail so that you and the trainee know exactly what is required. This also ensures that you evaluate each trainee using the same standards.

See example of Performance Assessment Checklist is on the next page.

59

Example of a Performance Assessment (criterion referenced) Checklist:

Name: _____   Date: _____

Machine Operator

Check Points	Check Point Performance		Maximum possible score	Actual Score	Pass or Fail
Mill first and second surfaces			**16**		
1. Select speed of cutter and feed of table.	Sat	Unsat	1		
2. Position end mill to right front of vise and mill side of block until clean	Sat	Unsat	5		
3. Remove block and debur.	Sat	Unsat	2		
4. Reinsert machined side against solid vise jaw, leaving about ½ inch extending beyond end of vise. Tighten top down.	Sat	Unsat	3		
5. Mill second side until clean.	Sat	Unsat	3		
6. Debur second side.	Sat	Unsat	2		
7. Dimensions (first two sides) are milled and square to .005.	Sat	Unsat			
Required Score to Pass			**11**		

Example of a Performance Assessment (criterion referenced) Checklist:

60

INSTRUCTIONAL METHODS

The selection of the appropriate instructional method(s) is dependent on the following factors:
- ➤ Learner
- ➤ The learning objectives (type, domain, and level)
- ➤ Availability of training materials i.e. videos
- ➤ Availability of learning facilities and equipment

The following table looks at the different instructional methods, their advantages and disadvantages, their intended purpose, and when to use them.

Method	Advantages	Disadvantages	Purpose	When to Use
Role Playing: Acting out real-life situations in a protected, low risk environment	Develop Skills Opportunity to practice what is learned Participants gain insight into own behavior.	Some participants resist. Contrived situations. Requires considerable planning	Help participants practice skills used in interactions.	To practice newly acquired skill. To experience what a particular situation feels like. To provide feedback to participants about their behavior.
Games: An activity governed be rules entailing a competitive situation.	Promotes active learning. Provides immediate feedback. Boosts interest. Increases learning. Improves retention.	Time consuming. May lead to loss of facilitator control. Sometimes difficult to monitor. Some degree of risk.	Provides non-threatening way to present or review course material.	To help gasp total program content. To present dry material in an interesting way. To add a competitive element to the session.
Simulations: Activity designed to reflect reality.	Promotes high level of motivation and participation. Provides immediate feedback. Approximates real world environment.	Can be costly. Time-consuming. Requires significant planning and excellent facilitation skills. May require more that one facilitator.	Recreates a process or event, or set of circumstances so that participants can experience and manipulate the situation without risk.	To integrate and apply a complex set of skills. To elicit participants' natural tendencies and provide feedback on those tendencies. To provide a realistic, job related experience.
Observation: Watching others without directly participating; then giving constructive feedback.	Generates interest and enthusiasm. Is less threatening than other methods. Promotes sharing of ideas and observations.	Focus could easily shift from learning to entertainment. Demonstrators may not do adequate job. Requires skilled facilitator.	Certain participants act out or demonstrate behaviors, tasks, or situations while others observe and give feedback.	To show group how to perform procedure or apply a skill or behavior. To increase participants' observation, critiquing, and feedback skills. To demonstrate behavior modeling.

Method	Advantages	Disadvantages	Purpose	When to Use
Instrument: Paper and pencil device used to gather information.	Personalized; helps to achieve participant buy-in and commitment. Helps focus on most appropriate material. Helps clarify theory, concepts, and terminology.	Some participants might be fearful. Participants might argue with data. Time-consuming. Requires skilled facilitator.	Provide feedback, self-assessment.	To identify areas for improvement. To establish a baseline for future growth.
Lecture: Short, structured, one-way communication from trainer to participants.	Trainer controls what material is covered. Saves time. Increases participation. Creates risk free environment.	***Participant passive mode.*** May be boring to participants. One-way communication.	Conveys information when interaction or discussion is not desired or is not possible.	To convey information quickly within a short period of time. To communicate same information to large people. To provide basic information to a group that is not knowledgeable.
Small Group Discussion: Small groups formed to discuss a certain topic within certain time limit.	Stimulates thinking. Draws on knowledge and experience of all group members. Helps participants to assess their understanding of material.	One participant might dominate. No guarantee that all will participate. No way to be sure everyone does under-stand. Time consuming. Easy for group to get "off-track".	Offers opportunity for participants to express opinions, share ideas, solve problems, and interact with others.	To generate ideas. To find out what participants think about a particular subject. To increase level of participation. To encourage group interaction and build group cohesiveness.
Case Study: Studying and solving a work related situation.	Everyone can participate. Particularly effective for shy participants.	Individual task; little or no interaction. Time consuming. Some may have aversion to writing.	Allow participants to discover certain learning points themselves.	To apply new knowledge to a specific situation. To practice problem-solving skills.

EXPERIENCE AND LEARNING

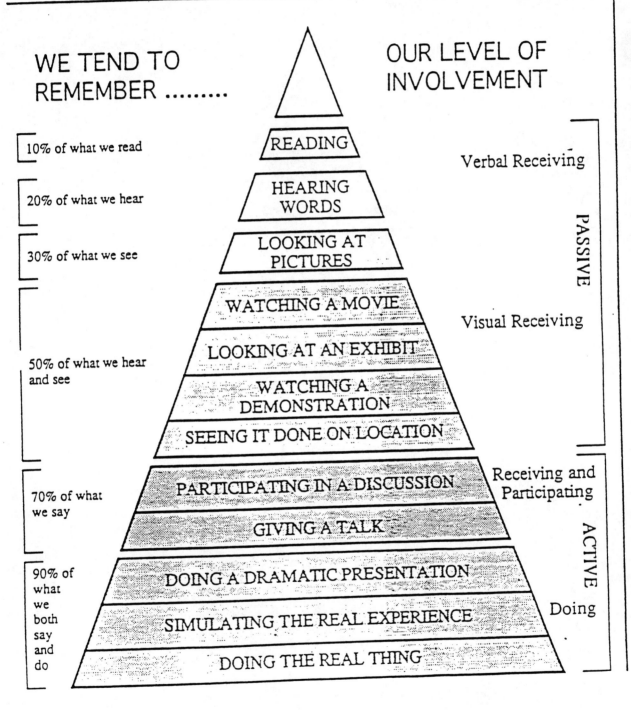

WE TEND TO
REMEMBER ....

OUR LEVEL OF
INVOLVEMENT

CONE OF LEARNING

developed and revised by Bruce Hyland
from material by Edgar Dale

10% of what we read

20% of what we hear

30% of what we see

50% of what we hear
and see

70% of what
we say

90% of
what
we
both
say
and
do

READING

HEARING
WORDS

LOOKING AT
PICTURES

WATCHING A MOVIE

LOOKING AT AN EXHIBIT

WATCHING A
DEMONSTRATION

SEEING IT DONE ON LOCATION

PARTICIPATING IN A DISCUSSION

GIVING A TALK

DOING A DRAMATIC PRESENTATION

SIMULATING THE REAL EXPERIENCE

DOING THE REAL THING

Verbal Receiving

Visual Receiving

Receiving and
Participating

Doing

PASSIVE

ACTIVE

63

MATCHING INSTRUCTIONAL METHODS TO DOMAIN AND LEVEL OF LEARNING

(A guide to help you select the best method of instruction based upon the type/level of learning required.)

DOMAIN & LEVEL OF LEARNING	MOST APPROPRIATE METHOD
COGNITIVE DOMAIN	
KNOWLEDGE	Lecture, Programmed Instruction, Drill and Practice
COMPREHENSION	Lecture, Modularized Instruction, Programmed Instruction
APPLICATION	Discussion, Simulations and Games, CAI, Modularized Instruction, Field Exercises
ANALYSIS	Discussion, Independent/Group Projects, Simulations, Field Experience, Role-playing, Laboratory
SYNTHESIS	Independent/Group Projects, Field Experience, Role-playing, Laboratory
EVALUATION	Independent/Group Projects, Field Experience, Laboratory
AFFECTIVE DOMAIN	
RECEIVING	Lecture, Discussion, Modularized Instruction, Field Experience
RESPONDING	Discussion, Simulations, Role-playing, Field Experience
VALUING	Discussion, Independent/Group Projects, Simulations, Role-playing, Field Experience
ORGANIZATION	Discussion, Independent/Group Projects, Field Experience
CHARACTERIZATION BY A VALUE	Independent Projects, Field Experience

64

PSYCHOMOTOR DOMAIN

PERCEPTION — Demonstration (lecture), Drill and Practice

SET — Demonstration (lecture), Drill and Practice

GUIDED RESPONSE — Peer Teaching, Games, Role-playing, Field Experience, Drill and Practice

MECHANISM — Games, Role-playing, Field Experience, Drill and Practice

COMPLEX OVERT RESPONSE — Games, Field Experience

ADAPTATION — Independent Projects, Games, Field Experience

ORIGINATION — Independent Projects, Games, Field Experience

65

ON – THE –JOB –TRAINING (OJT) MODEL
(Follow the 1 –2 –3 – 4)

Step 1: Preparation of the Leaner
- Put the learner at ease – relieve the tension
- Explain why he or she is being taught
- Create interest, encourage questions, and find out what the learner already knows about his/hers job or other jobs.
- Explain the why of the whole job and relate it to some job the worker already knows.
- Place the learner as close to the normal working position as possible.
- Familiarize the worker with the equipment, material, tools and trade items.

Step 2: Presentation of the Operation
- Explain quantity and quality requirements.
- Go through the job at the normal work pace.
- Go through the job at a slow pace several times, slowly, explaining each step. Between operations, explain the difficult parts, o those in which errors are likely to be made.
- Again go through the job at slow pace several times; explain the key points.
- Have the learner explain the steps as you go through the job at a slow pace.

Step 3: Performance Tryout
- Have learner go through the job several times, slowly explaining to you each step. Correct mistakes, and if necessary, do some of the complicated steps the first few times.
- You, the trainer, run the job at a normal pace.
- Have the learned do the job, gradually building up skill and speed.
- As soon as the learner demonstrates ability to do the job, let the work begin, but don't abandon them.

Step 4: Follow- Up
- Designate to whom the learner should go for help if he or she needs it.
- Gradually decrease supervision, checking work from time to time against quality and quantity standards.
- Correct faulty work patterns that begin to creep into the work, and do it before they become a habit. Also show why the learned method is superior.
- Compliment good work; encourage the worker until they are able to meet the quality and quantity standards.

66

Whole Brain Learning

1. The concept of _____ entails using teaching strategies that are developed for both sides of the brain.

2. Therefore, the product of whole brain learning is greater than the sums of it parts.

3. The brain is the _____ _____ of all learning activities.

4. The concept of _____ _____ means that we use one half of the brain to a greater extent than the other half. This makes us unique and gives us a specialized preference for learning specifically it determines our

   _____.

5. The brain is divided into halves referred to the Left and Right. It can be divided into four quadrants, with each having a specialized function. These are outlined below by how each section learns and how to teach to that section, therefore developing a Whole Brain Learning way of teaching.

Learning styles represented by the specialized modes of the four quadrants:

Cerebral Left Learns by: -Thinking through ideas -Values logical thinking -Needs facts -Forms theories -Builds cases	**Cerebral Right** Learns by: -Self-discovery -Constructs concepts -Values initiative -Is concerned with hidden possibilities
Limbic Left Learns by: -Testing theories -Values structure and process -Oriented to skill attainment through practice	**Limbic Right** Learns by: -Listening and sharing ideas -Values intuitive thinking -Works for harmony -Integrates experience with self

Design and delivery approaches for the specialized modes of the four quadrants:

Cerebral Left: -Formalized lecture, data based, case discussions, textbooks, program learning, and behavior modification	**Cerebral Right:** -Nonstructural, experiential, experimental, visual, aesthetic, individual, and involved.
Limbic Left: -Structured, sequential, lecture, textbook, organizational case discussions, programmed learning, and behavior modification.	**Limbic Right:** -Experiential, sensory involvement, musical, people-oriented, case discussions, and group-interactive.

Selecting Media for Training

Cost and efficiency are the keys to selecting the right instructional media for training.

By Jim Heideman

The goal of instructional media in technical training is to increase the efficiency of the learning process and the effectiveness of the training by making it easier or faster for trainees to attain the course's instructional objectives. Just as critically, the course's media must also be cost-effective for the organization.

Many studies have assessed various media, pointing out the comparative strengths and advantages of one instructional medium over another in knowledge retention, job performance, or other evaluative measures. But in many instances, it's difficult to use this research because the circumstances in these studies never quite seem to match what we face in training.

Perhaps we should accept all media as valid when they improve instructional efficiency and are cost-effective. Yet, many times we choose media for the wrong reasons and spend money on instructional media that do not improve instructional efficiency and are not cost-effective.

The following discussion presents a framework for media selection that will support your training, result in the greatest benefit for your trainees, and be the most economical.

Objectives Before Media

Instructional media can be as simple as a printed worksheet distributed prior to or during a lesson, or as complex as an interactive videodisk program taking hundreds of staff hours to produce and costing thousands of dollars. Despite the variety of media available, the selection process demands first that the medium selected must be consistent with the learning objectives.

Sometimes, however, there is confusion between a learning objective and an "activity" that appears to be an objective. For instance, consider a large retailer that wants to equip all its sales outlets with videotape players to introduce product innovations to its sales people. Once the hardware is in place, management proposes this "objective" for training: "By the end of this year, we will have produced and distributed 12 video programs that introduce the new product line to all our dealers."

While this sounds like an objective, it is really a statement of planned activities. Situations like this occur when an organization makes a strategic decision to invest in new training hardware and then feels it should support that decision. When activities rather than objectives drive instruction, the potential for efficient training is diminished because the selected media may not be the best instructional choice. Just as critically, organizational performance suffers because valuable resources are wasted on what may be unnecessary training media.

When you face training situations in which media are being selected, ask about the objective. Then ask yourself, "Do we really have a learning objective?"

Once you've determined the learning objective (or perhaps replaced the activity statement with a learning objective), you can refine the selection process further by identifying the type of learning objective the media will support. Different types of objectives require different levels of sensory involvement for your trainees. To identify an objective's type, use a taxonomy of objectives, such as the one developed by Robert Gagné. He identified five types of learning objectives, each related to a different learning outcome: intellectual skills, cognitive strategies, verbal information, motor skills, and attitudes.

In This Story

▼ Instructional systems design
▼ training materials design
▼ training technologies
▼ training systems

Technical & Skills Training ▼ Aug/Sept 1992

As an example of different learning outcomes, consider the following two objectives. While similar, each has a different type of learning outcome. The first objective addresses motor skills: "The trainees will be able to replace a vehicle's defective water pump."

As you decide on the media to use to support this objective, you will be making different decisions than you will for the second objective, which addresses intellectual skills: "The trainees will be able to determine when a vehicle's water pump is defective." This objective requires the trainees to discriminate between normal operation and faulty water pump operation.

In selecting media, remember that you are making selections based on the best sensory involvement for attaining the learning objective. Ask yourself six critical questions:

Does the objective require motion? In considering media that might be used to attain the above-mentioned motor skills' learning objective, motion could be used to model the removal and reinstallation procedure. Ask yourself if this is necessary. Because the objective has a motor-skill outcome and is procedural, you might choose instead to include a written instructional sheet with step-by-step procedures and drawings that illustrate what should be done at each step.

The second objective has an intellectual skill outcome requiring the trainees to discriminate between normal and faulty water pump operation. To master this objective, trainees will first need to inspect visually for water pump leaks and external defects. Second, trainees must discriminate between noises that indicate a defective water pump and noises that are normally present in a vehicle's engine compartment. The trainees' sensory involvement is both auditory and visual. The auditory element will not require motion. And because the visual inspection can be made under static conditions, motion will add little to the trainees' mastery of the objective.

Does the objective require color? When the major sensory involvement for an objective is visual, color can greatly increase instructional efficiency. In the first objective, if replacement parts are color-coded, use of media that are in color might help ensure that the trainees install the correct replacement part. If print material is used, color can add considerable cost. So consider using a chart that shows color-coding or separate text that identifies the colors. While adding color can increase the efficiency of trainees' mastery of the objective, don't ignore less expensive alternatives.

What degree of image resolution is required? High resolution enables your trainees to distinguish one image from another. With print media, for example, you will need to decide whether photographs have sufficient image resolution for your objective, or if line drawings would be better.

Resolution should also be considered when motion is required. A photo taken with a hand-held camera and available light will most likely have poorer resolution than a video produced by a professional video production company. In considering both print and motion media, be aware of the costs.

What degree of fidelity is required? Fidelity is the degree to which a sound is accurately reproduced. When considering the auditory aspects of the second objective above, for example, the sound must have high enough fidelity so that the sounds that indicate a bad water pump can be distinguished from normal engine compartment sounds. Without enough fidelity, trainees won't be able to master the performance required by the objective.

Fidelity also has a video dimension. In video, fidelity refers to how well the images represent the actual items that you are trying to portray. For example, if a piece of equipment is surrounded by so many other objects that it's hard to tell one piece from another, it might be better to use a line drawing of the object you are describing rather than showing film of the actual object in its cluttered environment.

How much variety needs to be built in? Since job performance may require trainees to face situation unlike those in training, pre-

senting a variety of examples during training will give trainees a more complete view of the job's activities. Consider the first objective. There are many types of water pumps on many different cars. Each vehicle has its own peculiarities of disassembly and reassembly. No single way affordably covers every conceivable situation, and it may not be necessary. Try illustrating general procedural steps, such as "drain cooling system."

How much reality is necessary? At times, using the real object is the only appropriate way to support your learning objective. All other media forfeit some reality in the interest of practicality. When you select media with lesser reality, you are compromising clarity but perhaps increasing efficiency and cost-effectiveness. Be aware of these trade-offs.

In the second objective, the highest degree of reality would require an example of every defect you want your trainees to identify. This requires a number of vehicles, each with a different problem. Logically, this is difficult and costly. More importantly, it is not essential for meeting the objective because other, more cost-effective methods are available. These include an audiocassette to give examples of typical noises that indicate a defect or a line drawing or illustration that indicates key locations for inspection.

Flexible Selections

Be flexible when you analyze the results of your selection process. Sometimes you will have several alternatives. The answers may even suggest a combination

of media for successful instruction. So be sure to make your choices based on the learning objective.

Your selection process is complete when you determine the costs of the media. Develop a best-case and one or two fallback positions.

Be prepared to discuss how each alternative will affect learning. And be prepared to balance your support for your training objectives with concern for organizational resources.

Even though each training situation is different, always consider the practicality of your decisions. If you focus on the learning objective, you can present well-thought-out recommendations to management. If you recommend that the organization spend thousands of dollars to train all instructors to use new hardware, or if you suggest that an entire

training center has to be redesigned to accommodate the rear projection video system that you are recommending, watch out!

A final note: Making the right decision for the right reasons can save time and money for your organization. More importantly, wise choices increase the efficiency and effectiveness of your training. And that enhances your credibility. ▼

References

Gagné, R.F. *Principles of Instructional Design.* New York: Holt, Rinehart and Winston, 1979.

Jim Heideman is a technical training project specialist for Nissan Motor Corporation. He may be reached at 10821 Holly Dr., Garden Grove, CA 92640, 714/530-5635.

70

INSTRUCTIONAL STRATEGY
(What is the best way to teach this?)

The Instructional Strategy is developed based upon the objectives you wish to accomplish, and contains two major parts: the Sequence Strategy and the Media Strategy. The first step in developing your Instructional Strategy is to determine in what order the objectives will be taught. This is called **"Sequencing"**. To determine what sequence is best for teaching your objectives consider the following:

Job Performance Sequence- the procedures or tasks are taught in the same order as they are done on the job.

Simple to Complex Cognitive Sequence- A progression that promotes understanding; known to unknown, simple to complex, concrete to abstract.

Logical Performance Sequence- A logical combination of the job performance elements and there desired order. Just makes more sense this way.

In determining which sequence to use, it helps to compare at least two different sequences to see which one makes the most sense and presents the training in the more understandable way. Once the sequence has been determined, a media strategy is determined for each objective.

The **Media Strategy** involves looking at each objective and then determining how best to teach it. This contains three parts:

Media - The media are the vehicles that carry information. Some examples of media are lectures, printed materials, books, pamphlets, handouts, films and slides, video, human interaction, demonstration, "realia" (the real thing) . . .

Consider: 1. What media best supports each training objective?

2. Is it an effective learning tool?

3. Will the cost be within your budget?

Strategy - What you as an instructor will do to get the material across using the above selected media. This includes the different instructional techniques of lecture, demonstration, etc. Consider what domain of learning your objective is in. See Matching Methods to Domain and Level of Learning.

Activity - What you expect the student to do in the learning process. Includes student demonstrations, answering questions, practicing procedures, etc.

71

ASSIGNMENT GUIDELINES

Take each objective and determine the media, strategy, and activity that are the best methods for teaching that objective considering time, cost, ease of learning, and availability of equipment.

Write out each objective: (You may summarize or write out the objective in long form.)

Example:

<u>Objective 1:</u>	Be able to identify (by listing) the four steps which should be taken in each of two restaurant emergency situations.
<u>Media:</u> (What supports instruction).	Printed handouts; Chapter 3, textbook <u>Restaurant Operations</u>
<u>Strategy:</u> (What the trainer will do)	Trainer will provide an independent study packet to trainees and explain the highlights of Chapter 3 from the identified textbook
<u>Activity:</u> (What the learner will do)	Trainees will complete the independent study packets after listening to the trainer's explanation of the highlights of Chapter 3.

Example:

INSTRUCTIONAL STRATEGY

Sequencing of teaching objectives: 1 3 2 5 7 4 9 8 6
Justification: Starting with the basic steps, then moving to the more complex material is the best sequence.

<u>Media Strategy</u>:

Objective 1: Identify the parts of a Lenox letter sorter.

Media: Wall charts and overhead transparencies of the parts.

Strategy: Lecture and discussion giving an overview of the parts of the Lenox letter sorter.

Activity: Students will be asked to identify parts of the Lenox, and to enter into a discussion as to what the parts are used for.

Complete a media strategy for each objective, see worksheet next page.

72

INSTRUCTIONAL STRATEGY WORKSHEET

Instructional Sequence:_____

Justification: _____

_____

Media Strategy:

Objective # 1: _____

_____

Media: _____

Strategy: _____

Activity: _____

Objective # 2: _____

_____

Media: _____

Strategy: _____

Activity: _____

Objective # 3: _____

_____

Media: _____

Strategy: _____

Activity: _____

Objective # 4: _____

_____

Media: _____

Strategy: _____

Activity: _____

Objective # 5: _____

_____

Media: _____

Strategy: _____

Activity: _____

Objective # 6: _____

_____

Media: _____

Strategy: _____

Activity: _____

73

ROUGH DRAFT OF FINAL MATERIALS
(Let's see how it all fits together.)

A "Rough Draft" is the first look at the final and complete training session you're designing. The rough draft gives you the chance to be creative - it should be the most fun part of the packet.

This is where you expand your INSTRUCTIONAL STRATEGIES assignment. Get as specific here as you can. Go through your entire training sessions from start to finish and give a rough sketch of the media, activities, presentations, job aids, etc. For example, if you need a poster as part of your training, draw out a rough draft of the poster on 8 1/2" x 11" paper and specify that it should be 3' x 2' or whatever size you decide (or draw it on the large paper if you want).

If you have role-play, specify how many people will be involved, what roles they will play, etc.

If you need a certain room arrangement, draw it out (layout).

If you need special tools, materials, equipment or supplies, provide a list.

For speeches or oral instructions, provide a rough draft of what you plan to say. How will you get the trainees involved? What will you do to grab their attention? Will you use an analogy, startling statistics, or humor? Specify!!! Do not just say you'll use an analogy and some surprising statistics - tell me exactly what you'll use.

If you'll have a handout or a job aid, give a rough drawing of what it will look like. Stick figures are OK.

Are you splitting the trainees into groups? How will you split them up - by work groups, job classifications, and birthdays?

For slide shows, videos, or Computer Based Training (CBT) use squares drawn on paper as storyboard cards. Draw what the slides, video segment, or computer screens will look like. Add the narration or background music if appropriate.

"Visualize your training program"
Room and Equipment Set-up

Preparation

Introduction   Icebreaker   Motivation of learners

Presentation
Take your Instructional Strategy and put it into visual format by roughing out what the handout, overheads, video, and other job aid will look like and how they will be used.

Application
How will the learner get to practice and/or apply these new skills? Map out how the simulation or practice session will run.

Evaluation
How and when will you evaluate whether they have learned as well as the process?

Look at the following example. Be creative and thorough.

ROUGH DRAFT

Introduction:
    Who we are
    What we do
    Why we are here

Preparation

    Posters of safety precautions
    Handouts, overhead transparencies,
    Prepare arm with lacerations,
    Bring CPR Annie, prepared CPR
    and First Aid tests, prepared First
    Aid packets, prepare written
    and skills safety test, bring props
    (goggles, hearing devices, gloves,
    Hat, and suit)

Icebreaker
    (Overhead)
    Facts:
        % of accidents on the job
        % of accidents on the farm
        % of accidents in the home
    Pictures of industrial accidents

    (Prop)
        Arm with laceration and bone sticking out.
Explain that most of these injuries could be prevented by safety training.   How to help others
who have been injured by using the first aid techniques.

Motivation
    Using above information and pictures to motivate trainee to desire knowledge about safety
    so they will not become a statistic   Initiate a desire for First Aid so they can help co-workers and
    family members who may become victims.

Equipment
    CPR Annie
    Posters
    Overhead machine
    Videos
    Survey
    Goggles
    Gloves

    First Aid packets
    Overhead transparencies
    Handouts
    VCR and TV
    First Aid & CPR test
    Hearing devices

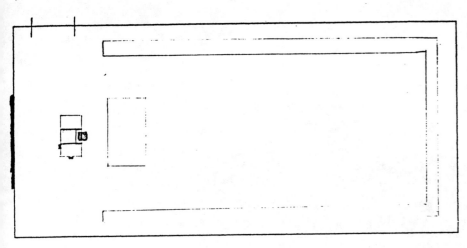

Room Arrangement
  Need:
Overhead
Table up front
Table and chairs in U-
shape with room in
between for a
demonstration.

Obj. 1 & 2

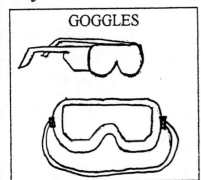

GOGGLES

Handout & overhead, lecture
presented by lecture and demo
Demonstrate how to check for clarity , how to apply goggles
comfortably and snug with a pair of goggles.
Have learner to repeat process until successful.

Obj. 3

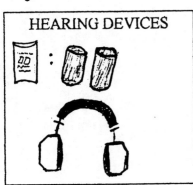

HEARING DEVICES

Handout and overhead, lecture
Presented by lecture and demo
Demonstrating how to correctly apply a hearing device that
will block out 60% of the noise.
Have learner to demonstrate procedure with 100 % accuracy

Obj. 6

Video, lecture
Purpose of hard hat, requirements of hard hat
Importance of labeling your hat
Learner must be able to answer questions accurately

Obj. 4 & 5

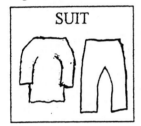

Handout, video, lecture
Give fit requirements, explain importance of proper fit
Demonstrate "suiting up" and know when to "suit up"
Learner must demonstrate knowledge about the suit.

Obj. 7

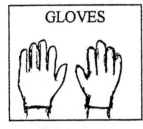

Handout, overhead, gloves
Demonstrate putting on and taking off the gloves properly
Explain why gloves are so important
Learner must properly complete the steps of putting on and taking off
the gloves without tearing the gloves

Obj. 9

CPR FIRST AID
• bleeding
• lacerations
• amputations
• burns & elec

Handout, overheads, video, lecture, tests (written & skills)
Trainer will lecture, demonstrate, and use overheads, CPR Annie,
study packets, and exams
Student will need to successfully demonstrate one-man CPR, pass
a CPR written test with an 84% or above, pass a written First Aid
test with an 85% or above, demonstrate the main procedures
taught in the First Aid portion with 90% accuracy

Obj. 8

Posters, handouts, lectures, video, test (written & skills)
Pictures of safety features and devices
Trainer will give knowledge of new standards of safety, proper use of safety equipment, knowledge of why safety is so important, and reasons why everyone should follow safety rules.
Student must receive 80% or higher on written test and miss no more than 4 steps on the skills test.

VIDEO

Role play having an employee using a saw without safety devices. Second employee steps in to correct first employee.

Employees exchange conversation on proper procedures. The employees will then demonstrate putting on the proper safety devices and explain why they are using them.

Next, will be a demonstration on one-man CPR on an Annie mannequin.

DEMONSTRATIONS:
applying goggles
applying hearing devices
selecting hard hat
"suiting up"
putting on and taking off gloves
one-man CPR
bandaging a laceration or broken bone

78

JOB AIDS / HANDOUTS

Job aids are training materials used on the job and are used to ensure that the trainee takes to the job the exact procedures and knowledge necessary to complete the task. Information that you do not what the trainee/employee to rely strictly on the memory to know. The most common and most useful functions of job aids are to help employees to remember information that is critical to doing a job and to learn procedures required to perform a job. Since job aids often extend and in sometimes replace training, they must be carefully designed to promote learning in an efficient and cost-effective manner.

Job aids have the following characteristics:

They tell or show what to do
They indicate when and in what order to do certain tasks
They define specific terms and use them in job-specific context
They are graphic more than narrative
They represent generic or standardized information
They are separate from other materials, and are often compact, sturdy, easy to use
They can be posted or distributed for broad use
They have simple instructions printed clearly on them

Below are some standard examples of different job aids:

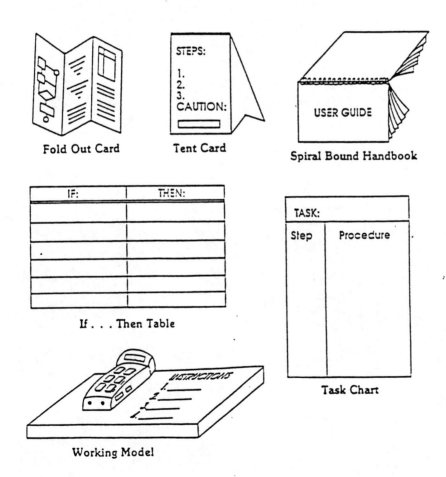

Fold Out Card   Tent Card

Spiral Bound Handbook

If . . . Then Table

Task Chart

Working Model

79

LESSON PLANNING
(Your guide while teaching.)

When planning a presentation or training session, the more thoroughly prepared and organized you are the better it will work. Lesson planning is a logical way to organize the information that you will be presenting in a format that will be easy for you to use and follow during the presentation. There are many different formats available: you need to select the one that is best for you. Most formats contain four sections:

Heading-- Lays out the general theme of the presentation, the total time needed, and equipment or materials needed.

Time Line--Lays out how much time is needed for each segment.

Main Points--Outline form of points you want to cover in the presentation. This should be outlined so that you can easily glance at the notes while talking. Avoid reading your notes out loud.

Methods, Media--Notes tied to specific main points to let you know what special points, media, demonstrations, etc. you intend to use to enhance that point.

The following is an example of one format of a lesson plan.

80

Lesson Plan Example:

Lesson Title: Interpreting Body Language

Purpose: Teach trainees how to interpret body language to detect dishonesty

General Plan: Use a brief lecture, video, role-play, and a quiz to teach and test trainees on how to interpret body language.

Time: 3 hours

Material/Media Needed: Brochures, training video, overhead transparencies, surprise gifts, extra writing utensils for trainees. Overhead projector, VCR and monitor

Time Line	Main Points	Media/Methods & Notes
10 min.	Introduction: Discuss the need to be aware of body language as it can signal dishonesty	Give pre-test. Show O?H of main objectives.
20 min.	Scenario: Supervisor is informed of a problem with dishonest employee; supervisor documents loss of money and determines if information is sufficient to approach suspected dishonest employee.	
10 min.	Demonstrate specific body language; 1. Eye contact 2. Lack of animation 3. Use of legs and arms 4. Touching of the face	Training video of scenario with deceitful body language portrayed.
30 min.	Supervisor interviews all employees involved with the loss; confirms suspicions and addresses solution to the problem.	
10 min.	Break	
30 min.	Application: Ask two volunteers to participate in role-play, have remaining trainees observe and practice interpreting body language; rotate participants if time allows.	Role-play; give surprise gifts to participants. Instructions for role-players and observers.
30 min.	Discussion of role-play	
30 min.	Evaluation: Give trainees a short quiz; review answers as a group. Ask trainees to complete an evaluation of the training session.	Answers on O/H
10 min.	Wrap-up: Explain benefits of the new skill just learned	

81

Lesson Plan Example

Lesson Title: Bagging Groceries

Purpose: To teach new employees how to select the proper bag and to correctly place grocery items into the bags. (This is basically the terminal objective).

General Plan: Use lecture and demonstration to show trainees how to bag groceries properly. Trainees will then practice bagging a variety of grocery items.

Time: 30 minutes

Materials: 10 - 12 varied grocery items and an assortment of bag sizes. Media needed: overhead projector, VCR and monitor, chalkboard.

Time Line	Main Points	Methods, Media, Notes
5 min.	Discuss the importance of proper bagging procedures, talk about store image, customer service.	Show video of irate customer and why. Show O/H of objectives.
10 min.	Bagging Procedures: 1. Select proper bag. 2. Open the bag. 3. Begin bagging as order is rung up. 4. Place large cans and bottles on bottom. 5. Put meats in plastic bags. 6. Put frozen foods in freezer bags. 7. Put bread on top. 8. Put "paid sticker" on items too big to bag.	Show different sized bags, cans, bottles, and boxes. Show freezer bags and "paid" stickers. Demonstrate proper bagging procedures.
10 min.	Application: Have trainees pair up and practice bagging groceries. Have trainees evaluate each other. Instructor will check each group then have other trainee bag the groceries.	Give 10-12 grocery items and bags to each group.
5 min.	Evaluation and wrap-up. Discuss what you observed as problems. Compliment group on accomplishment. Talk about unusual items and how to handle them. Open discussion on bagging procedures and problems. Stress importance of correct bagging procedures on customer satisfaction.	Video of store walk-through showing various items including unusual ones that need special handling.

82

LESSON PLAN WORKSHEET

Lesson Title: _____

Purpose: _____

General Plan: _____

_____

Time: _____(Total for lesson)

Material Needed: _____

_____

Time Line	Main Points	Media/Methods, Notes
_____	_____	_____
	_____	_____
	_____	_____
	_____	_____
_____	_____	_____
	_____	_____
	_____	_____
	_____	_____
_____	_____	_____
	_____	_____
	_____	_____
	_____	_____
_____	_____	_____
	_____	_____
	_____	_____
	_____	_____
_____	_____	_____
	_____	_____
	_____	_____
	_____	_____
_____	_____	_____
	_____	_____
	_____	_____

83

Using Training Videos

Video can be a very good instructional device, but the problem is that people are use to relaxing with TV. People use TV to unwind whole at home, often only devoting part of their attention while a video is playing. For a videotape to properly accomplish the task of instructing the learners, it needs to follow these suggestions:

- The video must first of all keep the vocabulary and visual effects simple. Research has found that people invest more effort in simple things. If information is complex, a person may miss important information while trying to understand it all.
- A good video will always make sure the message is central to the story and that there is a high degree of correspondence between the video and audio positions of the program.
- The instructor can help by informing the learners of what they need to learn from the video and can also provide questions for consideration during the presentation.
- The viewers can help themselves as well. " Before the video begins, ask the instructor what you're supposed to learn and how that fits into the course content.

Guidelines for evaluating a training video: (Connie Sasseen Bever, vice-president of American Media, Inc. offers these guidelines)

- Does the video meet your organization's learning objectives?
- Is the video appropriate for your organization's employees –their education and experience level, ages, and cultures?
- Is the work environment shown similar to yours?
- Does the video offer just the right level of information? Choose a video that aims towards the top; that way everyone will learn something.
- Does the video command attention with good pacing, dramatic audience involving situations, including empathy with the main characters, and lots of changes of scenes – or it dull?
- Are the characters and situations realistic and appropriate/
- Are the desired behaviors modeled in a way employees can emulate?
- Is there too much emphasis on the wrong behavior/
- Can employees identify with the characters that model desired behaviors or are the characters too perfect?
- Are the characters diverse—racial, gender, and in other ways?
- Is the content presented in a logical, easy to follow sequence or is it random?
- Does the video summarize key learning points with attention-getting visuals as it progresses/
- Is it the right length? For most audiences the video should more exceed 22 minutes unless there is a break.
- Is technical quality good, with clear sound and visuals, pleasing lighting correct color, and music that doesn't drown out the spoken word?

84

Video Specifications
(Guidelines for your video.)

The training video is an integral part of today's training programs. The quality of your video can enhance or detract from the quality of your training program, depending on how well it is done. Now that you are ready to add the video section of your training program, remember the following:

a. Good instructional videos come as a result of research and should enhance the overall training program.

b. Training videos should be simple, to the point, and fun to make.

c. They should relate directly to the overall training program of which they are a part.

Specifications for your video:

1. Lead in, music or other video, that is appropriate to the video and will motivate and bring reality to the training.

2. Title card with name of training, and authors of the video. Like the credits of a movie.

3. Introduction that covers what this training video is and why it is important. State the training objectives that are covered in the video.

4. Body that covers the training objectives in the sequence that you think is best suited to enhance learning.

5. Concluding remarks and closing, which summarizes key points. Emphasize what you really want them to remember.

6. Final closing credits if needed to give recognition to the video crew.

7. All team members must appear in the video.

8. Video is to be six to 10 minutes long. Less than six will lose points. More than 10 require instructor approval.

REMEMBER:

This is your chance to be creative, have fun, and produce a quality product. Add those things that will hold your attention and still be appropriate to the learning climate of your training session.

By Phillip J. Stella

Scriptwriting made easy or easier

Failing to plan is planning to fail.

Sound familiar? We've all been there — getting stressed out trying to slay the writers-block dragon. You can't use magic, technology or wishful thinking to fight that dragon, but you can use a secret weapon to make scriptwriting easy — well, OK, OK — easier.

Veteran scriptwriters know that the more effectively and thoroughly they plan and interact with clients, the easier and faster the actual writing process will be. The result? Delivering scripts on time that meet their standards and clients' needs as well. Secret For Success No. 2 — "Failing to plan is planning to fail in scriptwriting."

In order to sharpen that weapon, let's review and highlight the key steps in the video script-planning process, examining the critical effect that those steps have on writing the script.

Planning the script

• *Objectives*

The whole process begins with a thorough needs analysis — identifying the problem the video is supposed to solve, its specific objectives and audience specs. Script objectives should be viewer-based, clear, specific, achievable and measurable. Most videos include combinations of skill objectives (the viewer will be able to do something), knowledge objectives (the viewer will know something) and attitude objectives (the viewer will believe/feel something).

• *Audience*

Often more important than simple demographics is the audience's psychographic profile. What do the audience members feel about the topic now? How do you want them to feel after watching the video? Also consider how the audience feels about the messenger.

The earlier you can get involved in this needs analysis process, the better. It allows an in-depth review of all of the factors that will affect the outcome. Getting involved from step 1 helps ensure that you and your client will use the best idea you can think of, not the first idea you thought of or the idea you usually think of.

• *Alternatives*

Although video script-writers may make their living writing scripts, business communication professionals help clients determine the best way to solve their problems. After reviewing the specific objectives for the message and the audience profile, help your client determine the smartest solution. Video may not be the best solution, or there may not be enough time or budget to do video properly. The only thing worse than a bad video is a good video that should have been a meeting, brochure or memo.

Although you may think you're turning down business for yourself or your department, what you're really doing is helping your clients and increasing your credibility as a valued problem solver. Secret For Success No. 3 — "Always strive to help your clients solve their problems; that's the driving force behind our value."

• *Approach*

Once you've agreed that a video is a smart solution for your client's objectives, audience, budget and time line, brainstorm creatively and patiently to identify what tone, style, format and approach make the most sense. What will work for the client's needs, not your personal creative preferences? Secret For Success No. 4 — "Tone and style can overshadow content — and even interfere with communication."

Also, consider the relationship between the video and other key communication tools involved in the project. Video rarely delivers the total message. It works best in consort with other communications tools, each designed to accomplish a specific piece of the total project.

Here's another opportunity to help your clients. Although they may have come to you looking for

Scene No. 1 — Peter Andrews sits at his PC, staring at the monitor screen. It's blank except for the title "Employee Orientation Video, Draft No. 1." He looks at the clock, sips some coffee, scans his notes and comes back to stare at that blank screen. Muttering under his breath, he hopes the right words will almost magically appear. He hears the words he's said to clients so often echoing in his head: "Secret For Success No. 1 — 'A good script is absolutely critical to the success of any video project!'" Time passes slowly, very slowly. Peter sits, yawns and stares.

Stella is a free-lance writer, president of Effective Training & Communications, Mayfield Village, OH, and a founding member of ITVA/Cleveland.

a video script, you can advise them on other elements, such as print or meetings, as well. Secret For Success No. 5 — "You're not just a scriptwriter, you're a communication problem solver."

• *Content*

Next, identify what basic factual and visual information will accomplish your objectives. What do you need to show and tell the audience? How will you structure it? How will you explain or exemplify it? Involve your client heavily here as you outline content and identify resources together. You rarely have the time to learn everything possible about the subject yourself.

• *Proposal*

Turn the above planning details into a thorough, but succinct, proposal and rough storyboard. Use storyboarding software or simple pencil sketches. The client should be able to close his or her eyes and see the video.

Stress the importance of appropriate senior management sign-offs. They decrease the likelihood of downstream problems and force the client to stay involved in the project. Deal with the feedback you get with sensitivity, tact and common sense.

Scene No. 2 — Joe Foonman sits at his PC, quickly writing a script draft. He reviews his detailed proposal and script outline, talks through narration out loud and writes — fast. No writers-block dragon here.

Two weeks ago, he met with Ralph Norton, vice president of employee benefits, to plan the annual benefits communication campaign.

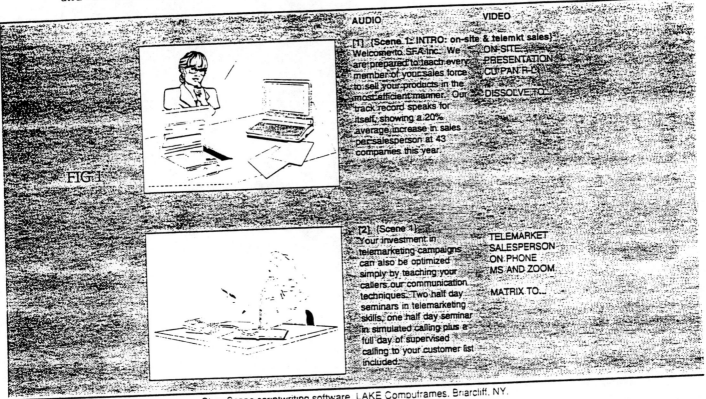

AUDIO

VIDEO

[1] {Scene 1: INTRO: on-site & telemkt sales}
Welcome to SFA Inc. We are prepared to teach every member of your sales force to sell your products in the most efficient manner. Our track record speaks for itself, showing a 20% average increase in sales per salesperson at 43 companies this year.

ON-SITE PRESENTATION
CU PAN R-L

DISSOLVE TO

[2] {Scene 1}
Your investment in telemarketing campaigns can also be optimized simply by teaching your callers our communication techniques. Two half day seminars in telemarketing skills, one half day seminar in simulated calling plus a full day of supervised calling to your customer list included.

TELEMARKET SALESPERSON ON PHONE
MS AND ZOOM

MATRIX TO...

FIG 1

Sample storyboard courtesy ShowScape scriptwriting software. LAKE Computrames. Briarcliff, NY.

They agreed to include several mailers sent to employees' homes, two newsletter articles and an hour information meeting with a video. It would summarize the key points previously raised, give some examples of benefit choices and review the enrollment instructions.

They defined specific objectives for the video and agreed on a simple talking head with graphic support approach, because of time and budget constraints and Ralph's conservative nature. Ralph agreed to include a teaser opening with several sound bites of employees asking questions about the benefits.

Rough write

With the planning details determined, visualization identified and structural framework created, you're well on your way. You should also be able to close your eyes now and see the finished video. Rather than staring at that blank screen, you simply start expanding your outline.

Because you're in a "brain dump" mode now, write as fast as you can. Use a Dictaphone to talk through the dialogue and narration — the talents will. Then transcribe it if that works for you. This will help you write conversationally, with active verbs and simple structure.

Secret For Success No. 6 — "Write like you speak — and write fast!"

Don't get hung up on word choice, style or even spelling. Just get the concepts from your head onto screen or paper. Leave holes for facts you can fill in later. When you're through the first pass, walk away from it — if only for an hour. Get a mental and emotional change of pace. Come back refreshed and ready to edit ruthlessly!

Editing

Before you begin editing and polishing, review your needs analysis decisions about objectives, audience, tone and content. Then pretend you're reading someone else's script. Is there enough of the right kind of detail and information to accomplish your objectives? Does the approach and format work? Is the language and tone appropriate for the audience? Fill in fact holes and check for grammar and spelling problems.

Read it aloud to see how it flows. Record it and listen to a playback to see how it sounds. Time the playback. If you're too long — and you probably will be — identify the "B" material or points that can be cut.

Avoid overly dense narrative — let the pictures do the talking. Turn the rough storyboards into more polished and complete visual treatments, based on graphics resources you have available.

Client review

Now you're ready to present your draft and storyboards to your client for review, comment and — with luck — sign-off. Because you did such a thorough job in the needs analysis and proposal, there should be few surprises — OK, OK, OK — fewer surprises.

Allow time for multilevel review and the usual political games that accompany this process. Resolve problems, differences of opinion or issues as efficiently and diplomatically as possible. However, don't let your creative writer's pride and sense of ownership interfere with good client relations and com-mon sense. Remember Secret For Success No. 7 — "It's the client's baby. You're really only the nanny."

I love this job!

At this point, you should have a final draft that accomplishes its objectives and meets — or exceeds — the client's expectations. With the proper planning, thorough needs analysis and effective storyboarding, you should have been able to slay — or at least seriously wound — the writers-block dragon.

Scene No. 3 — Joe Foonman sits at his PC, printing his invoice for Ralph Norton's benefits video script. He puts his feet up on the desk, sips some coffee and looks at his daily "to do" list. He also re-reads the glowing thank-you note Norton sent him about the script, with copies to his boss and the vice president of communications. As Joe straightens his desk and takes the rest of the afternoon off, he can't help but remember Secret For Success No. 8 — "You could have had a real job, but No! You had to work in show business instead!"

88

SCRIPT AND STORYBOARDING YOUR TRAINING VIDEO

Now that you have studied the training problem, written the training objectives, sequenced them and developed your instructional strategy you are ready to start the development of your video. Before you pick up a camera, carefully plan out your project. In your instructional strategy and rough draft you have determined what instructional points that the video will be used as the media to support the teaching process. The next step is to map out your video using script and storyboards.

The storyboard card is a visual and instructional tool used to lay out a scene either for video shooting or an instructional situation. In video shooting it contains three KEY elements that tell the camera operator what they are to do. Storyboards are normally written on 4 x 6 inch or larger cards for ease of use, or can be drawn on a half sheet of paper as shown below.

SCENE # 1

Filming Notes:
(This is what the camera operator is to film). Example: Wide angle shot of factory.

Action: (This is the action that is taking place in the scene. This lets the camera operator know what action to expect). Describing customer service in terms of survival for the business and all employees.

The SCRIPT is the actual words said by the actors. The scene numbers tie the script and story board cards together. By actually writing out what is to be said you can ensure that what you are saying is correct and in the context that the learner (viewer) will understand. The script provides a format that can be approved before filming to ensure that it contains a clear description of the material on which you are training. Careful preparation in this area can greatly enhance the effectiveness of a training video. Great video shots are not effective if the words say something else. The following is the format for the script:

SCENE # (ties it to a particular story board card)

Action: (What is happening in the scene.)
No action, film factory.
as introduction to employee
orientation video.

Narration: (Words being said by the actors.)
Fairfield is a nation wide producer of quality gear and components for large equipment. It is located in Lafayette, IN and employees 300 people.

STORY BOARD

Scene # _____

Filming Notes: _____

_____

_____

_____

Action:_____

_____

_____

_____

SCRIPT   Scene #_____

Action:_____

_____

_____

_____

Narration:_____

_____

_____

_____

_____

_____

_____

_____

_____

_____

Page _____ of _____

TRAINER AND CONTENT EVALUATION
(What did they think of the training and how it was presented?)

Evaluation of the instructional process and the course content is an important aspect of any training program. There is no "perfect" course, just as there is no "perfect" instructor. Making instruction better is the instructor's responsibility. In order to do that, a feedback system needs to be developed to get valid and useful information from which to assess the course as well as the instructor's delivery skills. **Formative evaluation** is an on-going process throughout the training process. Waiting until the end of training to evaluate could mean that you wasted your training time. Decide what you want to know about how your content is being received and the method you are using to deliver it.

ASSIGNMENT GUIDELINES

1. Determine what feedback information you need to make a valid assessment of the course.

2. Determine what feedback you would like concerning your teaching skills.

3. Develop at least five questions to measure the course content and at least five questions to measure your teaching skills.

4. Establish a standard format for these questions that contains a rating scale.

5. In addition to a standard rating scale for questions, you can also use open-ended questions for more in-depth information.

6. Develop a Trainer/Content Evaluation instrument using the following example as a guide.

EXAMPLE: TRAINER/CONTENT EVALUATION

To each of the following questions circle either:
1. Strongly Disagree
2. Disagree
3. Undecided
4. Agree
5. Strongly Agree

	SD	D	U	A	SA
1. The material fit my needs.	1	2	3	4	5
2. The material was easily understood.	1	2	3	4	5
3. The material was well organized.	1	2	3	4	5
4. The trainer made me feel comfortable.	1	2	3	4	5
5. The trainer was well prepared.	1	2	3	4	5

6. Etc. for a total of at least 10 questions....
7. What additional material would you have liked to have seen?

_____

8. What would have made your learning easier?

_____

91

TRAINING PRESENTATION PROCEDURES
(Presentation procedures may vary by instructor.)

The following procedures will be used for the Training Program presentations. You are a training team so divide the responsibilities between partners. For each presentation the following will be needed.

      1. Your completed training packet.
      2. Five copies of your two handouts. These will be given to the observers.

PRESENTATION PROCEDURES

- Introduce yourselves

- Introduce your topic and motivate the learner, conduct an icebreaker if appropriate

- Conduct training involving the class in the learning
  - Utilize your media (handouts, video, and transparencies) in your training.

  - Involve the class in the learning process through exercises, simulations, and/or discussions.

  - Introduce and use your video/simulation as part of the training process.

  - At the end of training summarize key points then have students fill out training evaluation forms.

- Critique procedures
  The instructor will be evaluating
  - your training procedures
  - your use of media
  - the quality of your training media
  - how you involved the learners in the training process
the quality of your training program

- Students will fill out the critique sheets at the end of the presentation and turn them in to the instructor. Comment sheets are for feedback to the presenters and will be included along with the instructor's grade sheet in your training packet when it is returned. This will give the presenters differing points of view as to how their training was received.

92

TRAINING SESSION GRADING STANDARDS
(Items and point values may vary with instructor.)

NOTES

GENERAL (25)	Pts	Total
Professionalism	5	
Enthusiasm	5	
Appropriate introduction of presenters and topic	5	
Classroom set-up	5	
Demonstrated the need for training	5	
	25	
INTERACTION/PARTICIPATION (45)		
Incorporated a "Hands-on" participative approach (H,S,D)	10	
Simulation/Activity well organized with clear instructions	5	
Learner/Instructor Contact	5	
Tone, voice projection, gestures, note reading	5	
Q & A	5	
	30	
MEDIA / CONTENT (55)		
Appropriate intro to activity/simulation/video	5	
Handouts appropriate, neat, useful, and support topic	10	
Overhead transparencies appropriate, readable, and support topic	10	
Quality of video and other support materials	10	
Management of media	5	
Quality of training content	15	
Learning objectives incorporated into presentation	5	
	60	
TRANSITIONS (10)		
Transitions between presenters.	5	
Transitions between segments	5	
	10	
OVERALL (45)		
Creativity	10	
Conclusion / Summary	5	
Meets time guidelines (Minus 5pts ea. Minute under)	5	
Learners level of interest	5	
	25	
Total Available Points	150	

93

Team Member Evaluation Form (Mid Semester)

_____

Your Name   Class time/Section

To be filled out and turned as requested by the instructor. This form is used midway through the semester and again after your final presentation.

- The scale is 0 – 5, with 5 being the best possible assessment.
- An average will be taken to calculate total score of group member responses.
- A grade of 0 will be assigned for evaluations not turned in.
- The total possible points for this evaluation are 20.
- For each group member put their name, circle a value, and justify if needed.

Used the following scale;
No participation = (0)
Attended meeting with average input and participation = (3)
Active team involvement, excellent input = (5)

Group Member Name: _____   0 –1 –2 –3 –4 – 5
Comments:

_____

Group Member Name: _____   0 –1 –2 –3 –4 – 5
Comments:

_____

Group Member Name: _____   0 –1 –2 –3 –4 – 5
Comments:

_____

Group Member Name: _____   0 –1 –2 –3 –4 – 5
Comments:

_____

94

Team Member Evaluation Form
(After Final Presentation)

_____

Your Name   Class time/Section

To be filled out and turned as requested by the instructor. This form is used midway through the semester and again after your final presentation.

- The scale is 0 – 5, with 5 being the best possible assessment.
- An average will be taken to calculate total score of group member responses.
- A grade of 0 will be assigned for evaluations not turned in.
- The total possible points for this evaluation are 20.
- For each group member put their name, circle a value, and justify if needed.

Used the following scale;
No participation = (0)
Attended meeting with average input and participation = (3)
Active team involvement, excellent input = (5)

Group Member Name: _____   0 –1 –2 –3 –4 – 5
Comments:

_____

Group Member Name: _____   0 –1 –2 –3 –4 – 5
Comments:

_____

Group Member Name: _____   0 –1 –2 –3 –4 – 5
Comments:

_____

Group Member Name: _____   0 –1 –2 –3 –4 – 5
Comments:

_____

*A crash course for the novice trainer on how to conduct
a good seminar.*
....

THE PEDAGOGUE'S DECALOGUE

BY FRANK O'MEARA

Maybe you're a manager. Maybe you're a team leader. Maybe you're a technician. Whatever the case, you know enough about *something* that somebody in the organization has decided you ought to pass on the knowledge. Congratulations, you're going to conduct a seminar.

To get off on the right foot, please consider the following 10 rules, a sort of "pedagogue's decalogue." They won't make you an instant expert in the art and science of teaching, but they can help you avoid some major pitfalls. If nothing else, perhaps they can serve as a reminder to keep your attention focused where it belongs: on the learners.

I. CHANGE YOUR SHOES.
....

No doubt you have encountered some teachers, professors or learned experts who seemed to believe otherwise, but the point of a training session is not to prove the instructor's competence or to display her knowledge and experience. The point is to make sure that these resources help the participants deepen *their* knowledge and develop *their* competence.

The purpose of teaching is learning.

Learning doesn't happen simply because an instructor delivers a speech, however well-constructed, on a subject in which he is an expert. Learning happens when a concept, an aptitude or a body of knowledge is understood, assimilated and mastered by the learner. That is why a good teacher begins by imagining himself as a member of his audience, by seeing his subject from the learners' point of view, and by asking some basic questions:

- What does my audience already know about the subject?
- What is their experience in this area?
- What do they need to know about it?
- What do they want to know about it?
- What importance do they attach to it?
- What are their likely questions, difficulties and misconceptions about it?

Your answers to these questions will help you prepare the module you are going to teach. But what really matters is *their* answers to those questions. Before you go any further, try to find out what your audience knows and thinks about the subject. You

might ask them, survey them, test them, watch them on the job, talk to their supervisors—whatever gives you the information you need to help you focus your module on their real needs, on their understanding, on their learning.

II. GET YOUR ACT TOGETHER.
....

You know your stuff. You also know what the audience needs to know about your subject. And you have a time frame in which to get your message across.

The first thing to decide in preparing your session is, what are the three or four main things you want these people to learn? Be careful here: Whatever you're trying to teach, there is a world of difference between what you think would be good to explain to them, and what you want them to be *capable of* at the end of the session.

What do you want them to know, to understand, to remember, to be convinced of and to be able to *do*? Furthermore, how are you going to know they know? It all starts with the way you phrase the objectives. The trick is to build into your objectives the criteria by which you can observe and thus evaluate the knowledge and know-how that your trainees have acquired. If you're teaching people how to change a tire, your objective is not just to impart information about tire changing, but to see to it that by the end of the session, everybody can, in fact, successfully change a tire. We'll come back to this point later in the decalogue.

For the moment, just remember to think of the content of your module not in terms of chapter headings, but in terms of operational and observable competencies: At the end of the day, participants will be able to define, recognize, explain, distinguish, analyze, use or do whatever it is you set out to teach them.

The next thing is to plan the overall structure of your module. A seminar day can be divided handily into four blocks: two in the morning, two in the afternoon (the important thing about coffee breaks is the break, not the beverage). In a full-day seminar you can wrap up each unit of the module in one and a half to two hours, and increase your chances of retaining participants' attention and interest with a change of pace as you tackle each new

Illustrations by Tom Foty

*Until they tell you, show you
and do it themselves,
they have not acquired the knowledge or mastered the skill
you want them to learn.*
....

unit.

Finally, plan the day using a three-column outline: objectives, content and methodology.

The objectives will correspond to the principal competency for each of the time slots during the day. The content column will flesh out the main messages of each unit. The methods column will list the choices you make as to the ways learning will happen (explanation, discussion, simulations, group work, individual responses to questionnaires, etc.), as well as the visual or audiovisual aids you plan to use. This one-page outline of the day will help you keep the whole picture in focus. It will prompt you to build in cohesion, continuity, variety and active participation. The participants' ability to assimilate information and develop skills will depend, in large measure, on the clarity of the plan you construct.

III. LOOSEN UP.
....

Yes, this seminar is serious business. You have a lot of material to convey, and you have a plan that is a model of time management. You've no time to waste on chitchat. You're not interested in delivering a prima donna performance or gathering votes as the year's jolliest instructor.

On the other hand, seminars need not be a pain in the neck. As a participant, you probably remember best—and learned most in—sessions in which the instructor took the time to break the ice. If you're like most of us, you prefer an instructor whose style is businesslike but relaxed, one who makes you feel you can speak up without busting a schedule set in concrete.

Be attentive to the groups' reactions. Change gears whenever you notice signs of incomprehension, boredom or fatigue. Hang loose. And smile.

IV. UNCOMPLICATE IT.
....

This subject you're teaching is perfectly clear to you. You know it inside out. What's not clear sometimes is why things are not obvious to others.

It's up to you to make sure participants have the vocabulary to understand what you're talking about. The advantages of a *hyperlogographic* reading of company procedures rather than a *hypologographic* reading may be self-evident to you, but the audience might be excused for not sharing your conviction. In other words, express your ideas in the simplest possible language.

Follow the advice of Cicero, who suggested that without examples nothing is taught and nothing is learned.

Your technical explanations should be accompanied by visual representations (pictures, graphs, drawings) or simulations of real-life situa-

tions. Better yet, wherever possible, provide direct contact with the thing you are talking about.

The assimilation of cognitive input is in inverse proportion to the presence of obfuscation. That's a complicated way of saying: If you want them to understand, express your message as clearly, as vividly and as simply as possible.

V. PUT IT ON ICE.
....

We've spoken of the need for a certain flexibility in presenting your material. You've prepared your program. You've mapped out the itinerary for the day. Now you need to motivate your participants, to make them feel it's *their* program.

One way is to begin by letting them know what you plan to cover, and then inviting them to let *you* know what questions they might have about those subjects. Put these questions on ice: Write them on a flip chart and promise to integrate them into your presentation, or at least to answer them in an open forum before the end of the day. This signals your participants that other questions will be welcomed during the session, that you aim at having them assimilate a certain amount of prepared material, but that you intend to make communication a two-way affair.

After all, there's little point in spending the day telling them what they could read in a book or your lecture notes. The specific pedagogical advantage of a seminar is that it permits dialogue with the instructor and within the group. Exploit it.

VI. VARY YOUR PITCH.
....

An instructor ought to be comfortable with several different teaching techniques so as to maintain and renew interest and participation during the day.

The predictable format for a training module is: formal presentation by the instructor, followed by questions from the audience or perhaps an exercise in small groups, and then synthesis and conclusion by the instructor. That's one way. Here are half a dozen others:

- *Demonstration.* Show them how to fill in a form, how to conduct an interview, how to analyze information, how to construct a budget or whatever.

- *Simulation.* Invite two individuals to assume the role of client and salesperson, manager and subordinate—whatever is appropriate. Ask the other participants to observe and comment on the simulated experience. Or ask some members of the group to take part in a simulated staff meeting that the others analyze with the help of observation sheets.

In some cases, you may want to use a video recorder to tape the role players so they can evaluate their own performance.

- *Case study.* Present a documented, real situation for analysis by the group or by subgroups.

People dislike the hypocrisy of flattery,
but they do like to be respected for who they are,
for what they already know, for what they can do
and for their ability to learn.

• *Discussion.* Break the participants into small groups. Have them share their ideas on some topic or question you have posed. Ask them to present the results to the rest of the group.

• *Individual tasks.* Ask each participant to fill in a questionnaire, to analyze a document or to explain a particular point to the group.

• *Group projects.* Ask small groups to produce a document or a series of transparencies or flip charts that can be used in a final segment at the end of the session.

The important thing is to realize that while lectures can be useful and even necessary in a seminar, they need not be the only item on the menu.

VII. LET GEORGE DO IT.

You can tell them, you can show them, you can do it for them. But until they tell you, show you and do it themselves, they have not acquired the knowledge or mastered the skill you want them to learn.

Active participation is not just a way of keeping people awake and busy. It is the way adults learn.

If you spend 75 percent of the day talking, you can be sure *you* will have a better grasp of your subject. If, on the other hand, you let them work on a problem, let them discover how to do it, let them explain what they have learned, let them apply their knowledge, let them learn by doing, then you can be sure *they* will get the hang of it. Which is the whole point, remember?

VIII. PLAY IT AGAIN, SAM.

"Repetitio mater lectionis" is how Cicero put it. Repetition is the mother of learning.

They may have heard you the first time, but they'll understand it better the second time, especially if you find a different way to express it (visually, for instance). And when they hear it the third time, you will have made sure that it's one of them who's doing the talking.

If they hear it, see it, say it and do it...then, by George, they've got it.

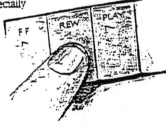

IX. ACCENTUATE THE POSITIVE.

Teaching is a tricky business. If we were dealing with tape recorders rather than people, it would be relatively simple. Tape recorders absorb everything they hear, and it makes no difference whether they actually "understand" a word of it. Moreover, they're sensitive to sound, but devoid of emotions. They need no motivation, no encouragement, none of the niceties of interper-

sonal communication.

People are different. They don't like to be embarrassed, made fun of or treated like morons. They dislike the hypocrisy of flattery, but they do like to be respected for who they are, for what they already know, for what they can do and for their ability to learn.

A wise instructor will not hesitate to recognize ignorance or to correct misunderstanding. But he will be patient and positive in trying to ensure each individual's comprehension and proficiency.

Always try to underline what's correct in an imperfect answer or performance before pointing out what's wrong or needs to be improved. That's not a moral imperative, it's a pedagogical one.

X. GET A RECEIPT.

We've said it all along: The point of your seminar is to make sure participants know what they're supposed to know.

Making sure does not necessarily mean administering a test at the end of the day.

Throughout the seminar, you've been aiming at operational and observable competencies. You built into your objectives the criteria for evaluating those competencies. When observers are capable of finding what's wrong or in need of improvement in a simulated sales call, when individuals or subgroups can summarize the material you've presented, when participants chosen at random can explain about products or procedures, when they show you they can *do* what you set out to make them capable of doing, you have the right to feel you have done your job.

You *know* they know.

POSTSCRIPT

Just in case you're still wondering what those weird words in "Uncomplicate It" mean, here are the definitions:

• *Hyperlogographic:* Characteristic of a reading by a normally educated person who spontaneously attributes meaning to words and groups of words without analyzing their phonetic structure.

• *Hypologographic:* Characteristic of a reading by a person who laboriously identifies each word by identifying each of its phonetic elements (letters or syllables).

You can now add an 11th commandment to your Pedagogue's Decalogue: "Tie up the loose ends." [T]

Frank O'Meara is a director at the Université (training center) of Cap Gemini Sogeti in Behoust near Paris. Cap Gemini Sogeti designs and manufactures computer software.